Jesus Christ: Saviour, Healer, Deliverer, LORD

Chris A. Legebow

ISBN-978-1-988914-08-4

DEDICATION

I thank God for the churches I have been a part of as well as Christian Broadcasting that has given me important foundations of our Christian Faith. I pray the book will help you to know Jesus Christ more deeply.

CONTENTS

ACKNOWLEDGMENTS

All Scripture taken from Biblegateway.com
Modern English Version (MEV)
.

1 INTRODUCTION

Jesus Christ: Saviour, Healer, Deliverer LORD

There are millions of people who know that Jesus Christ is their Saviour. They know they are sinners; they know that without forgiveness of Jesus Christ, they would not have relationship with God. As sure as the statement is true, there are millions of people who do not know that Jesus Christ is the Saviour. They don't know why they need a Saviour. There are people in North America who have not heard the gospel presented to them so that they can understand it. My book is written to give Biblical evidence of why Jesus is our Saviour and why we need a Saviour.

As sure as some do not know Jesus as Saviour, there are Christians who know Jesus as Saviour but do not know the truths of Jesus as Healer. Some churches do not preach healing in the name of Jesus. Some churches do not practice prayer and anointing with oil of the sick so that they may be healed. Many sincere Christians live without receiving divine healing because they do not know the same Jesus that died to save us also died so we might be healed. It is essential that the truths of Jesus as healer be taught and preached in our churches so that people would believe God for Divine healing.

There are Christians who do not know they do not have to be in bondage to any sin or addiction. Jesus triumphed over death, hell and the grave. What that means is that there is nothing that can bind you in addiction. Jesus Christ sets you free. It is the resurrection power of Jesus Christ that delivers people from addictions. There are well meaning Christians who spend all their lives claiming to be an alcoholic. Although I respect all types of ways of helping people be free from addictions, the truth can set you free, so you do not label yourself as an addict to anything. Rather, you give glory to God for your deliverance. Just as Jesus cast out demons and healed people in the scriptures, He does it today. Jesus commanded his disciples to preach the good news of salvation, healing and deliverance to all people. As Christians, these truths should be so evident in our lives that we preach them, do them and are recognized as Christians by people who are not Christians because of the evidence in our lives.

Mark 16: 15 He said to them, "Go into all the world, and preach the gospel to every creature. 16 He who believes and is baptized will be saved. But he who does not believe will be condemned. 17 These signs will accompany those who believe: In My name they will cast out demons; they will speak

1

with new tongues; 18 they will take up serpents; if they drink any deadly thing, it will not hurt them; they will lay hands on the sick, and they will recover."

My book will give evidence for Jesus as Saviour, as Healer and as Deliverer and LORD. It is my hope and my prayer that God may use the scriptures to quicken you to believe God's Word for complete blessing — life in the abundance of God's presence and covering. God is a rewarder of those who seek Him; He is a rewarder of those who have made covenant with Him.

2 JESUS THE SAVIOUR

Chapter 2

There is no one who has not sinned. The origin of sin is in our spiritual DNA. There is original sin in every person because we inherit it from Adam and Eve. God created man and woman to be holy and to live in his presence sharing, talking, having divine relationship with Him. We were created for God's glory and so that God may have a family. We were made in the image of God: both male and female. Adam and Eve enjoyed communion with God and direct access to God speaking with Him each day. God created all things to be a blessing and to live in harmony with mankind. Adam and Eve were clothed with God's presence. They lived naked but unashamed because they had God's spirit with them. It was innocence to evil and only knowledge of the good – only knowledge of God. God gave mankind a free will. That is each person can choose to live for God or to choose something else. Any other choice than God is not God's best. God's best is what is the best for man. If only we knew it, we would live it.

Adam and Eve did not know what God's words meant "If you eat of it, you will surely die." They did not know death or evil. They did not know there was any other type of life than living in the blessing of God. All they could possibly want was in the garden of Eden. There were trees full of fruit all around them; nuts, berries, all kinds of pleasant things. There was no thorn, no weed, no thistle; there was only perfection. Truly even at our best possible life, none of us has known that special relationship that Adam and Eve had with creation. Adam named all the animals. When the serpent talked with Eve, she wasn't frightened. I believe mankind was meant to communicate with animals. They lived in harmony. There was no shedding of blood. I'm sure they were vegetarians until the first sin that entered the world.

There was one tree, the tree of the knowledge of good and evil that God commanded Adam they should not eat of. God also attached a penalty to it. It was the only things they were not to partake of or they would surely die (Genesis 3: 2). Free will means they could disobey God; God would allow them to choose evil. God told them the clear consequence; if there had been no tempter, it is not known if man would disobey God.

Satan was thrown out of heaven for his pride and his arrogance towards God. Satan was once known as Lucifer, a beautiful mighty angel that overshadowed God's thrown giving God all the praise and worship of creation. He was powerful; he was beautiful, but all of his worth came from him fulfilling his purpose: to give all worship and praise to God. Lucifer also had free will. Within himself arose pride and a desire to keep the worship that was only for God. His arrogance grew, and he desired to overtake God's thrown by force. One third of the angels were with him. His beauty and his fall is described in the scriptures below.

Ezekiel 28: You had the seal of perfection,
  full of wisdom and perfect in beauty.
13 You were in Eden,
  the garden of God;
every precious stone was your covering:
  the sardius, topaz, and the diamond,
  the beryl, the onyx, and the jasper,
  the sapphire, the emerald, and the carbuncle, and gold.
The workmanship of your settings and sockets was in you;
  on the day that you were created, they were prepared.
14 You were the anointed cherub that covers,
  and I set you there;
you were upon the holy mountain of God;
  you walked up and down in the midst of the stones of fire.
15 You were perfect in your ways
  from the day that you were created,
  until iniquity was found in you.
16 By the multitude of your merchandise,
  you were filled with violence in your midst,
  and you sinned;
therefore I have cast you as profane out of the mountain of God;
  and I have destroyed you, O covering cherub,
  from the midst of the stones of fire.
17 Your heart was lifted up
  because of your beauty;
you have corrupted your wisdom
  by reason of your brightness;
I cast you to the ground,
  I lay you before kings, that they may see you.
18 You have defiled your sanctuaries
  by the multitude of your iniquities, by the iniquity of your trade;

Because of Lucifer's sin, pride and desire to overthrow God, he and the angels with him were thrown out of heaven into the atmosphere of the earth. Their punishment was banishment from God forever. They that saw God in his glory fought against God. Lucifer lost his title and his role and was now referred to in the scriptures as Satan, the enemy of God and man. Because Satan knew the man and woman in the garden were communing with God, Satan hated them. He desired to ruin their relationship with God. Satan possessed one of the animals, the serpent. The serpent tempted Eve by using some of God's words and causing Eve to doubt the goodness of God. He caused her to question God's word. The woman naively answered him saying that they could eat of any tree but the tree of the knowledge of good and evil. She said they could not even touch it or they would die; she is not quoting God accurately.

Genesis 3: 3 Now the serpent was more subtle than any beast of the field which the Lord God had made. And he said to the woman, "Has God said, 'You shall not eat of any tree of the garden'?"

2 And the woman said to the serpent, "We may eat of the fruit from the trees of the garden; 3 but from the fruit of the tree which is in the midst of the garden, God has said, 'You will not eat of it, nor will you touch it, or else you will die.'"

Sin Against God

The serpent again twisted God's words and lied about God saying that if she ate of the tree she would not die but would in fact be like god knowing good and evil. He tempted her with not only the fruit itself but the possible consequence that it could give her power to know good and evil; perhaps it caused her to doubt God's goodness towards her. She did not know she was being deceived by the serpent. She did know what she was doing though as she lusted after the fruit of the tree of the knowledge of good and evil,

Genesis 3: 4 Then the serpent said to the woman, "You surely will not die! 5 For God knows that on the day you eat of it your eyes will be opened and you will be like God, knowing good and evil.

The woman saw the fruit desirable. She liked the way it looked. She was no longer seeing it through God's eyes but rather through lust for it. She took it and partook of it and gave some to her husband who was there with her. Immediately they knew they were naked. I believe they had a covering of God's presence of God's glory on them and at that moment they sinned, they saw things as sinners. They were ashamed. They were filled with fear. These were feelings never intended for mankind. They were the direct result of sin against God.

Genesis 3: 6 When the woman saw that the tree was good for food, that it was pleasing to the eyes and a tree desirable to make one wise, she took of its fruit and ate; and she gave to her husband with her, and he ate. 7 Then the eyes of both were opened, and they knew that they were naked. So they sewed fig leaves together and made coverings for themselves.

The truth was Adam and Eve were only the first humans. All other humans are related to them. That original sin they committed changed the DNA of their bodies. They had not been created to die. Because of their sin, death, sin, the results of sin entered the earth. All people ever born have that original sin as part of our identity. It is less than what God wants for us. There was judgement on the serpent, the woman and the man.

Judgements of sin

The serpent had to crawl on its belly. I believe it lost its legs. It became an enemy of people.

Genesis 3: 14 The Lord God said to the serpent: "Because you have done this,
You are cursed above all livestock,
    and above every beast of the field;
you will go on your belly,
    and you will eat dust
    all the days of your life.

Even in uttering His judgements, God is merciful and offers a ray of hope that a seed of the woman will bruise the serpent's head. This is a direct reference to Jesus the Messiah who would come and defeat the devil, death, hell and all the curses of sin.

Genesis 3: 15 I will put enmity
    between you and the woman,
    and between your offspring and her offspring;
he will bruise your head,
    and you will bruise his heel."

The judgement on the woman is also harsh as she would now know pain in bearing children and in her husband ruling over her. No longer was she his equal. Only Jesus could defeat that curse making of all one in Messiah, both male and female.

Genesis 3: 16 To the woman He said,
"I will greatly multiply your pain in childbirth,
    and in pain you will bring forth children;
your desire will be for your husband,
    and he will rule over you."

The curse on Adam was also harsh. God cursed the earth because of him. God let thorns and weeds and other types of thistles infest the ground. Now labour would be hard for man. Man was sentenced to die. They did not physically die immediately but the sentence of death was upon them and also, they died spiritually. They no longer had access to \God. They no longer had relationship with God.

Genesis 3: 17 And to Adam He said, "Because you have listened to the voice of your wife and have eaten from the tree about which I commanded you, saying, 'You shall not eat of it,'

Cursed is the ground on account of you;
    in hard labor you will eat of it
    all the days of your life.
18 Thorns and thistles it will bring forth for you,
    and you will eat the plants of the field.
19 By the sweat of your face
    you will eat bread
until you return to the ground,
    because out of it you were taken;
for you are dust,
    and to dust you will return."

Original Sin

God replaced their sown-on fig leaves with animal skins. I believe the first blood sacrifice was offered that day to make atonement for their sin. As Lucifer was thrown out of heaven for his sin against God, Adam ad Eve were thrown out of the garden of Eden for their sin. No longer did they talk with God. They lost relationship with God and as a result, their children did not know God.

7

Genesis 3: 23 therefore the Lord God sent him out from the garden of Eden, to till the ground from which he was taken. 24 He drove the man out, and at the east of the garden of Eden He placed the cherubim and a flaming sword which turned in every direction, to guard the way to the tree of life.

The children born to Adam and Eve were many. As a result of that first sin, sin nature was passed on to all people born on earth. Cane their son killed his brother Abel because he was jealous and angry at God. Violence and evil were predominant in the earth so that within several chapters of Genesis, God decides to kill all people; He regrets creating people. But Noah, found favour with God. Hundreds of years later only one family, the family of Noah and the animals he brought with them into the ark lived. All other wicked people were destroyed. Only Noah chose to seek God and serve Him.

God makes covenant with Noah

God made a covenant with Noah and all the people and animals of the earth. Noah was given dominion of all the earth and all creatures and he was told to reproduce and prosper. Through Noah comes a new hope for man. The rainbow in the sky is a sign of the covenant that God made with Noah and all people and all animals.

Genesis 8: 15 Then God spoke to Noah, saying, 16 "Go out of the ark, you and your wife, and your sons and your sons' wives with you. 17 Bring out with you every living thing of all flesh that is with you, birds and animals, and every creeping thing that creeps on the earth, so that they may breed abundantly on the earth and be fruitful and multiply on the earth."

Murder is forbidden. A person who kills must be killed. God clearly commandments Noah to live by it and to teach others. The rainbow in the sky is a visible symbol of God's promise not to destroy the earth or all the people as long as the earth remains.

Genesis 9:

Whoever sheds the blood of man,
   by man shall his blood be shed;
for God made man
   in His own image.

7 And as for you, be fruitful and multiply; increase abundantly in the earth and multiply in it."

8 Again God spoke to Noah and to his sons with him, saying, 9 "As for Me, I establish My covenant with you, and with your descendants after you; 10 and with every living creature that is with you, the birds, the livestock, and every beast of the earth with you; of all that comes out of the ark, every beast of the earth. 11 I establish My covenant with you. Never again shall all flesh be cut off by the waters of a flood. Never again shall there be a flood to destroy the earth."

12 Then God said, "This is the sign of the covenant which I am making between Me and you and every living creature that is with you, for all future generations. 13 I have set My rainbow in the cloud, and it shall be a sign of a covenant between Me and the earth. 14 When I bring a cloud over the earth, the rainbow will be seen in the cloud; 15 then I will remember My covenant, which is between Me and you and every living creature of all flesh, and the waters will never again become a flood to destroy all flesh. 16 The rainbow will appear in the cloud, and I will see it and remember the everlasting covenant between God and every living creature of all flesh that is on the earth."

Abraham: God uses Him to birth a nation

Hundreds of years later, Abraham found favour with God. He lived among idol worshippers in Ur of the Chaldees. He did not know God until one day, God spoke to him clearly and gave him instruction. Abraham obeyed God. I truly believe that Abraham wanted to know the true living God so God revealed Himself to him. God commanded him a tough thing. He had to leave all that he knew, including all his family so that God could give him a new land. It required faith. It required obedience. Even though he was probably financially doing well where he was, he obeyed. He was approximately 70 years old. To leave all that he knew would have been tough. God's idea of revealing and giving him a new land was a unique promise. It was not something any one else ever knew. It was God's special promise to him.

Genesis 12:
1 Now the Lord said to Abram, "Go from your country, your family, and your father's house to the land that I will show you.
2 I will make of you a great nation;
  I will bless you

and make your name great,
   so that you will be a blessing.
3 I will bless them who bless you
   and curse him who curses you,[a]
and in you all families of the earth
   will be blessed."

Abraham fully obeys God and God leads his life and makes covenant with him. Genesis 13 explains God's promise to bless him with a large number of descendants even though Abraham and Sarah had no children yet. Part of the blessing is that God would raise up a people who lived holy unto God and become the nation of Israel, God's chosen people. As a sign of God's covenant with Abraham, all males had to be circumcised. It was their obedience to God.

Genesis 13: 14 After Lot had departed from him, the Lord said to Abram, "Lift up now your eyes, and look from the place where you are, northward and southward and eastward and westward. 15 All the land that you see I will give to you and to your descendants forever. 16 I will make your descendants like the dust of the earth, so that if a man could number the dust of the earth, then your descendants could also be numbered. 17 Arise, and walk throughout the land across its length and its width, for I will give it to you."

Through Abraham, his most unusual life with a miracle birth at the age of nearly 100, Abraham's descendants began. They became the nation of Israel. Through Israel came the promise of Messiah or the deliverer of the people.

Moses: Deliverer of Israel

Moses was born as an Israelite in Egyptian captivity. The descendants of Abraham were made to be slaves in Egypt for 400 years. There was to be a killing of all the first-born sons of Israel. The Egyptians feared prophecies telling about the deliverer who would set Israel free from their slavery. Moses was placed in a basket that was sealed with tar and placed in the river with a prayer that God would spare his life. He was found by a daughter of Pharaoh and for 40 years raised as a Prince in Egypt. Moses finds his true identity as an Israelite and defends an Israelite who was being beaten by an Egyptian.

Unwisely, Moses kills the Egyptian. He left Egypt fearing punishment for his crime. He finds Midian and becomes a Shepherd for 40 years with

Jethro. He has children. He seems to have discovered a good life. One day, God gets his attention and commandments Moses to go deliver the Israelites from Egyptian bondage. Moses reluctantly obeys but with the help of his brother Aaron. Through plagues upon the Egyptians and protection of Israel and a multitude of miracles, Israel is set free from bondage. The last plague in Egypt was the death of the first born. On that evening, God made a covenant remembrance for all of Israel – the Passover. It was to be taught to all the children of Israel until the end of the world. Each part of the Passover ceremony is important. Jesus fulfills the prophecy by giving his own life to be the lamb that would cleanse all of Israel and all people who would believe from their sins.

Passover regulations given to Moses: to Israel

Exodus 12: 17 You shall observe the Feast of Unleavened Bread. For on this very day I brought your armies out of the land of Egypt. Therefore you shall observe this day throughout your generations as an ordinance forever. 18 In the first month, on the fourteenth day of the month at evening, you shall eat unleavened bread until the twenty-first day of the month at evening. 19 Seven days shall there be no leaven found in your houses, for whoever eats that which is leavened, that person shall be cut off from the congregation of Israel, whether he be a stranger or born in the land. 20 You shall eat nothing leavened. In all your dwellings you shall eat unleavened bread.

21 Then Moses called for all the elders of Israel and said to them, "Draw out and take for yourselves a lamb according to your families and kill the Passover lamb. 22 You shall take a bunch of hyssop, and dip it in the blood that is in the basin, and apply the lintel and the two side posts with the blood that is in the basin, and none of you shall go out from the door of his house until the morning. 23 For the Lord will pass through to kill the Egyptians. And when He sees the blood upon the lintel and on the two side posts, the Lord will pass over the door and will not permit the destroyer to come to your houses to kill you.

24 "And you shall observe this thing as an ordinance to you and to your sons forever. 25 When you enter the land which the Lord will give you, according as He has promised, that you shall observe this service. 26 And when your children shall say to you, 'What does this service mean to you?' 27 that you shall say, 'It is the sacrifice of the Lord's Passover, who passed over the houses of the children of Israel in Egypt, when He smote the Egyptians, and delivered our households.'" And the people bowed down

and worshipped. 28 Then the children of Israel went and did so. Just as the Lord had commanded Moses and Aaron, so they did.

The Tenth Plague: Death of the Firstborn

Exodus 12: 29 At midnight the Lord smote all the firstborn in the land of Egypt, from the firstborn of Pharaoh that sat on his throne to the firstborn of the captive who was in the dungeon and all the firstborn of livestock. 30 Pharaoh rose up in the night, he and all his servants and all the Egyptians, and there was a great cry in Egypt, for there was not a house where there was not someone dead.

The next day, there were many first born who died. Israel got together quickly and left Egypt taking spoils of silver and gold from the Egyptians. The Exodus

Exodus: 31 Then he called for Moses and Aaron at night and said, "Rise up, and get out from among my people, both you and the children of Israel, and go, serve the Lord, as you have said. 32 Also take your flocks and your herds, as you have said, and be gone, and bless me also."

33 The Egyptians urged the people, so that they might send them out of the land in haste, for they said, "We all will be dead." 34 So the people took their dough before it was leavened, with their kneading troughs being bound up in their clothes on their shoulders. 35 Now the children of Israel did according to the word of Moses, and they requested of the Egyptians articles of silver and articles of gold, and clothing. 36 And the Lord gave the people favor in the sight of the Egyptians, so that they gave them what they requested. Thus they plundered the Egyptians.

37 Then the children of Israel journeyed from Rameses to Sukkoth, about six hundred thousand men on foot, besides children. 38 A mixed multitude also went up with them along with flocks and herds, a large amount of livestock. 39 They baked unleavened cakes of the dough which they brought forth out of Egypt, for it was not leavened because they were driven out of Egypt and could not linger, nor had they prepared for themselves any food.

40 Now the sojourning of the children of Israel who lived in Egypt was four hundred and thirty years. 41 And at the end of the four hundred and thirty years, on the very day, all the hosts of the Lord went out from the land of Egypt. 42 It is a night to be observed to the Lord for bringing them out from the land of Egypt. This is that night for the Lord to be observed

by all the children of Israel in their generations. It is significant because the blood of the lamb that placed on their doors and window seals represents the blood of Jesus the Messiah who would be born thousands of years later. It was the promise of the Messiah they were getting in the Passover celebration.

The Ordinance of Passover

Exodus 12: 43 So the Lord said to Moses and Aaron: This is the ordinance of the Passover:

No foreigner may eat of it. 44 But every man's servant bought with money, when you have circumcised him, may eat it. 45 A foreigner or a hired servant shall not eat it.

46 In one house shall it be eaten. You shall not carry any of the flesh outside of the house, nor shall you break a bone of it. 47 All the congregation of Israel shall keep it.

48 Now when a stranger sojourns with you and keeps the Passover to the Lord, let all his males be circumcised, and then let him come near and keep it. And he shall be as one that is born in the land. However, no uncircumcised person shall eat of it. 49 The same law shall apply to him that is a native and to the stranger who sojourns among you.

Exodus 12: 50 So all the children of Israel did it. They did just as the Lord commanded Moses and Aaron. 51 And that same day the Lord brought the children of Israel out of the land of Egypt by their hosts.

Death of the first born

Egypt's loss of the first born, including the firstborn of Pharaoh is enough to get Pharaoh's hardened heart softened. He lets Israel go and they take silver and gold from their captors.
After their escape from Egypt, Moses lead Israel to mount Sinai the place where he first met God. It is there that God gives to Israel the commandments. It is significant because God not only makes covenant with a person, Moses but with all of Israel. This is a direct response of blessing of God's people. This is a direct reverse of the curse of Adam.

God gives Moses the Commandments

Moses and Israel are God's people and God gives them the commandments, rules to live by that are pleasing to God. If man would obey these laws, their lives would be prosperous. God would bless them and they would prosper in all areas of life, including long life, health, finances, abundance, fertility etc.

It would have been important even if God had simply spoken the things to Moses to write. God believes they are so important to us that He Himself writes them on the side of a mountain and carves the tablets out of the stone and gives them to Moses. The finger of God, writing God's commandments is a special symbol of God's covenant with Israel.

The commandments cover both man's relationship with God and man's relationship with people. They are rules to live by. They are essential to living in covenant with God.

Exodus 20: 1 Now God spoke all these words, saying:

2 I am the Lord your God, who brought you out of the land of Egypt, out of the house of bondage.

3 You shall have no other gods before Me.

4 You shall not make for yourself any graven idol, or any likeness of anything that is in heaven above, or that is in the earth beneath, or that is in the water below the earth. 5 You shall not bow down to them or serve them; for I, the Lord your God, am a jealous God, visiting the iniquity of the fathers on the children to the third and fourth generation of them who hate Me, 6 and showing lovingkindness to thousands of them who love Me and keep My commandments.

7 You shall not take the name of the Lord your God in vain, for the Lord will not hold guiltless anyone who takes His name in vain.

8 Remember the Sabbath day and keep it holy. 9 Six days you shall labor and do all your work, 10 but the seventh day is a Sabbath to the Lord your God. On it you shall not do any work, you, or your son, or your daughter, or your male servant, or your female servant, or your livestock, or your sojourner who is within your gates. 11 For in six days the Lord made heaven and earth, the sea, and all that is in them, and rested on the seventh day. Therefore the Lord blessed the Sabbath day and made it holy.

12 Honor your father and your mother, that your days may be long in the land which the Lord your God is giving you.

13 You shall not murder.

14 You shall not commit adultery.

15 You shall not steal.

16 You shall not bear false witness against your neighbor.

17 You shall not covet your neighbor's house; you shall not covet your neighbor's wife, or his manservant, or his maidservant, or his ox, or his donkey, or anything that is your neighbor's.

God's Commandments

God also gave to Moses instructions for worship. Please see it was something unique and special. It is through Israel that God starts worship and praise and a holy priesthood through Aaron and his descendants the Levites. God gives Moses instructions for building a Tabernacle and an Ark of the Covenant which was a huge box overlaid with gold. God's presence would abide on the mercy seat of the ark. There were a total of 613 Levitical laws.

Please understand why the laws are so important. Israel had been in slavery for 400 years. Israel did not know freedom. Similar to Adam and Eve, they had free will but with original sin. The laws govern all aspects of life for the people. There are rules that govern treating people kindly, doing business properly, caring for the poor or the strangers etc. All aspects of human life are covered. It was to be the books of Moses or the Torah that were to be a foundation of the nature of Israel.

Sacrifices

Animal sacrifices were necessary for certain situations. If a person sinned or was giving thanks to God or practically any request from God or dealing with God, offerings were made. Animal sacrifices were to cover the sin until the Messiah would come. There was promise and hope. The Levites taught the people the laws and taught them to worship God. God's presence was in the midst of His people. A cloud of visible glory covered the ark of the covenant and over the tabernacle. God's presence was once more with God's people.

The Mosaic covenant meant that man could be set free from the curse of the law by relationship with God and by keeping the commandments. Even though they were free, even though they knew God had delivered them, even though they had seen the miracles of God, mankind still sinned. They were God's chosen people, but they had to offer sacrifices for sin. Man was not yet delivered from the curse of sin itself. The promise of the Messiah was that He would come and give His life as an offering for sin and that like the lamb's blood of Passover, his blood would not only cover, but erase the sins of the people giving them access to God.

Hundreds of years later, the prophet Isaiah uttered a promise of the coming Messiah who would give his life as a ransom.

Isaiah 53: Surely he has borne our grief
   and carried our sorrows;
Yet we esteemed him stricken,
   smitten of God, and afflicted.
5 But he was wounded for our transgressions,
   he was bruised for our iniquities;
the chastisement of our peace was upon him,
   and by his stripes we are healed.
6 All of us like sheep have gone astray;
   each of us has turned to his own way,
but the Lord has laid on him
   the iniquity of us all.

7 He was oppressed, and he was afflicted,
   yet he opened not his mouth;
he was brought as a lamb to the slaughter,
   and as a sheep before its shearers is silent,
   so he opened not his mouth.

Jesus Christ

Jesus miraculous birth and life are discussed throughout the gospels. The main point I am stating is that Jesus is the Messiah. He came to earth to save us from our sins, not only the result of sin, but He set us free from the bondage to sin. Jesus the living Word of God (instead of being written on a stone tablet, was living the word of God in his life) came to dwell with us on earth. God Himself took on human form and lived as one of us, without sin so that we who believe in him could have eternal life. He is identified as the Messiah by the Prophet John the Baptist who gets a prophetic revelation of Jesus and proclaims it.

John 1: 14 The Word became flesh and dwelt among us, and we saw His glory, the glory as the only Son of the Father, full of grace and truth.

John 1: 29 The next day John saw Jesus coming toward him and said, "Look, the Lamb of God, who takes away the sin of the world. 30 This is He of whom I said, 'After me comes a Man who is preferred before me, for He was before me.' 31 I did not know Him, but for this reason I came baptizing with water: so that He might be revealed to Israel."

32 Then John bore witness, saying, "I saw the Spirit descending from heaven like a dove, and it remained on Him. 33 I did not know Him, but He who sent me to baptize with water said to me, 'The One on whom you see the Spirit descending and remaining, this is He who baptizes with the Holy Spirit.' 34 I have seen and have borne witness that He is the Son of God."

Jesus: the Saviour

Jesus lived with his family until he was 30 years old. He was a carpenter. At 30, he was baptized by John the Baptist and a symbol like a dove appeared over him. He was the visible witness of the mercy of God towards man. Through faith in Jesus, as the Messiah, all people can be saved or redeemed to God which means people can once more speak directly with God and be at peace with God and live holy lives.

Romans 10: 13 For, "Everyone who calls on the name of the Lord shall be saved."[f]

Jesus was born of Mary a miracle – holy – lived a holy life.

At 30 for 3 years preached the kingdom of God and that He is the way th truth and the life.

John 14: 6 Jesus said to him, "I am the way, the truth, and the life comes to the Father except through Me. 7 If you had know would have known My Father also. From now on you do kr have seen Him."

Jesus healed people

Mark 10: 46 Then they came to Jericho. And as He went out of Jericho with His disciples and a great number of people, blind Bartimaeus, the son of Timaeus, sat along the way begging. 47 When he heard that it was Jesus of Nazareth, he began to cry out, "Jesus, Son of David, have mercy on me!"

48 Many ordered him to keep silent. But he cried out even more, "Son of David, have mercy on me!"

49 Jesus stood still and commanded him to be called.

So they called the blind man, saying, "Be of good comfort. Rise, He is calling you." 50 Throwing aside his garment, he rose and came to Jesus.

51 Jesus answered him, "What do you want Me to do for you?"

The blind man said to Him, "Rabbi, that I might receive my sight."

52 Jesus said to him, "Go your way. Your faith has made you well." Immediately he received his sight and followed Jesus on the way.

Jesus raised the dead

John 11: 21 Martha said to Jesus, "Lord, if You had been here, my brother would not have died. 22 But even now I know that whatever You may ask of God, God will give You."

23 Jesus said to her, "Your brother will rise again."

24 Martha said to Him, "I know that he will rise again in the resurrection on the last day."

25 Jesus said to her, "I am the resurrection and the life. He who believes in Me, though he may die, yet shall he live. 26 And whoever lives and believes in Me shall never die. Do you believe this?"

27 She said to Him, "Yes, Lord, I believe that You are the Christ, the Son of God, who is to come into the world."

Jesus the resurrection

Jesus revealed himself as the resurrection and the life to people who were mourning the death of their brother. Lazarus, a friend of Jesus had died. Jesus arrives there, and his sisters are in grief over his death. Both of them say to Jesus they know that Jesus could have healed Lazarus. Jesus proclaims the following:

Resurrection life John 11: 25 Jesus said to her, "I am the resurrection and the life. He who believes in Me, though he may die, yet shall he live.

John 14: 6 Jesus said to him, "I am the way, the truth, and the life. No one comes to the Father except through Me. 7 If you had known Me, you would have known My Father also. From now on you do know Him and have seen Him."

He says He is life more than once in the scriptures. In this passage he proclaims He is the resurrection. All of Israel was hoping and living believing that at the resurrection they would be judged by the laws but with mercy. All Israel knew the day of resurrection and judgement would follow. By speaking that He is the resurrection and the life, He demonstrates it by raising Lazarus from the grave. He demonstrates His proclamations by the miracles that are throughout his ministry.

Although Jesus only did good, preaching and healing and doing miracles, he was hated by the religious leaders. They were jealous of him and they sought for ways to catch him and kill him. Since they did not have the authority to kill him because they were in Roman occupation, they go to the Romans requesting his death.

Jesus did miracles – multiplication of loaves and fishes

John 6: 5 When Jesus looked up and saw a great crowd coming to Him, He said to Philip, "Where shall we buy bread that these may eat?" 6 He said this to test him, for He Himself knew what He would do.

7 Philip answered Him, "Two hundred denarii[a] worth of bread is not sufficient for each of them to receive but a little."

8 One of His disciples, Andrew, Simon Peter's brother, said to Him, 9 "There is a boy here who has five barley loaves and two small fish. But what are they among so many?"

10 Jesus said, "Make the people sit down." Now there was much grass in the place. So the men sat down, numbering about five thousand. 11 Jesus

then took the loaves, and when He had given thanks, He distributed them to the disciples, and the disciples to those who were sitting down; and likewise, they distributed the fish, as much as they wanted.

12 When they were filled, He told His disciples, "Collect the fragments that remain, that nothing may be lost." 13 So they collected them and filled twelve baskets with the fragments of the five barley loaves which were left over by those who had eaten.

14 When those men saw the sign which He had done, they then said, "This is truly the Prophet who is to come into the world." 15 Therefore, knowing that they would come and take Him by force to make Him king, Jesus departed again to a mountain by Himself alone.

Jesus only did good throughout his life.

Acts 10: 38 how God anointed Jesus of Nazareth with the Holy Spirit and with power, who went about doing good and healing all who were oppressed by the devil, for God was with Him.

Jesus commissioned disciples to preach salvation, healing and deliverance.

Same Jesus lives in believers today. It is our personal commission as well.

Mark 16: 15 He said to them, "Go into all the world, and preach the gospel to every creature. 16 He who believes and is baptized will be saved. But he who does not believe will be condemned. 17 These signs will accompany those who believe: In My name they will cast out demons; they will speak with new tongues; 18 they will take up serpents; if they drink any deadly thing, it will not hurt them; they will lay hands on the sick, and they will recover."

The Eternal Saviour

Jesus is Saviour past, present and future of all people – sacrifice once and for all. Because Jesus is holy, and He kept all the commandments, He gave his life as sacrifice for each person who would believe in him. God sees the believer in Jesus covered by Jesus blood, meaning that there is no sin because Jesus died for us so we might be the righteousness of God in Christ.

Hebrews 7: 24 But He, because He lives forever, has an everlasting priesthood. 25 Therefore He is able to save to the uttermost those who come to God through Him, because He at all times lives to make intercession for them.

Hebrews 7: 26 For such a High Priest was fitting for us, for He is holy, innocent, undefiled, separate from sinners, and is higher than the heavens. 27 Unlike those high priests, He does not need to offer daily sacrifices—first for His own sins and then for the people's, for He did this once for all when He offered up Himself. 28 For the law appoints men who are weak as high priests, but the word of the oath, which came after the law, appoints a Son who is made perfect forever.

All sin and iniquity can be forgiven – Jesus cleanses so it is if you never sinned. Jesus righteousness is our righteousness as we believe in him. We can commune with God because Jesus made a way by offering his own life to pay the penalty of sin.

Romans 3: 23 For all have sinned and come short of the glory of God, 24 being justified freely by His grace through the redemption that is in Christ Jesus, 25 whom God has set forth to be a propitiation through faith, in His blood, for a demonstration of His righteousness, because in His forbearance God had passed over the sins previously committed, 26 to prove His righteousness at this present time so that He might be just and be the justifier of him who has faith in Jesus.

Romans 5: 18 Therefore just as through the trespass of one man came condemnation for all men, so through the righteous act of One came justification of life for all men. 19 For just as through one man's disobedience the many were made sinners, so by the obedience of One the many will be made righteous.

20 But the law entered, so that sin might increase, but where sin increased, grace abounded much more, 21 so that just as sin reigned in death, grace might reign through righteousness unto eternal life through Jesus Christ our Lord.

Jesus always forgives

Jesus was tempted in all areas of life, but he did not sin. He is holy. He has kept all of the commandments. No other person could do it. He is God; he is man. He preached the good news to people that their sins could be forgiven. Jesus forgave sins while he was on the earth because He is God and has the authority to do it. Jesus lived holy.

Hebrews 4: 14 Since then we have a great High Priest who has passed into the heavens, Jesus the Son of God, let us hold firmly to our confession. 15 For we do not have a High Priest who cannot sympathize with our weaknesses, but One who was in every sense tempted like we are, yet without sin. 16 Let us then come with confidence to the throne of grace, that we may obtain mercy and find grace to help in time of need.

Jesus Ministry

The Apostle Peter summarizes Jesus fulfilling of the prophecies by his words.

Acts 2: 30 But being a prophet, and knowing that God had sworn with an oath to him, that of his seed according to the flesh, He would raise up the Christ to sit on his throne, 31 he foresaw this and spoke concerning the resurrection of the Christ, that His soul was not abandoned to Hades, nor did His flesh see corruption. 32 God raised up this Jesus, of which we all are witnesses. 33 Therefore being exalted to the right hand of God, and having received from the Father the promise of the Holy Spirit, He has poured out this which you now see and hear. 34 For David has not ascended to the heavens, yet he says:

'The Lord said to my Lord,
    "Sit at My right hand,
35 Until I make Your enemies
    Your footstool." '[c]

36 "Therefore, let all the house of Israel assuredly know that God has made this Jesus, whom you have crucified, both Lord and Christ."
Jesus is unjustly accused, abused, beaten, given to the Romans for punishment of death.

The New Covenant

Jesus died, was buried and rose again.

After the resurrection, Jesus gave that authority to preach the good news of salvation, healing and deliverance to his disciples.

Mark 16: 15 He said to them, "Go into all the world, and preach the gospel to every creature. 16 He who believes and is baptized will be saved. But he who does not believe will be condemned. 17 These signs will accompany those who believe: In My name they will cast out demons; they will speak with new tongues; 18 they will take up serpents; if they drink any deadly thing, it will not hurt them; they will lay hands on the sick, and they will recover."

Jesus forgives all sins and iniquities

Accepting Jesus as Saviour means that you realize you are a sinner. You recognize that the sin of Adam is in you and you can sin easily. You desire relationship with God which means you will pray, confess any sin to Jesus and receive his blood as forgiveness for you. The blood of the lamb, Jesus the Messiah was shed so that you could live forever in God's presence. God is Holy. God could not keep relationship with Adam and Eve because they were sinners. The Saviour Jesus wasn't born until 6,000 years later. God was merciful to man. He made covenant with Abraham. He made covenant with Moses. He raised up a nation of Israel descendants of Abraham as he promised he would do. He sent the Messiah Jesus that anyone who truly believes in him will be saved.

Jesus is the Saviour. Jesus blood shed for us gives us life. He died in my place so that I may have eternal life with God. Any sin of any person can be forgiven if the person will truly repent and turn to God.

Acts 16: 31 They said, "Believe in the Lord Jesus Christ, and you and your household will be saved."

1 John 1: 9 If we confess our sins, He is faithful and just to forgive us our sins and cleanse us from all unrighteousness.

Salvation for all not only Israel but Gentiles

Galatians 3: 26 You are all sons of God by faith in Christ Jesus. 27 For as many of you as have been baptized into Christ have put on Christ. 28 There is neither Jew nor Greek, there is neither slave nor free, and there is neither male nor female, for you are all one in Christ Jesus. 29 If you are Christ's, then you are Abraham's seed, and heirs according to the promise.

Romans 11 – Gentiles grafted in Jesus – heirs of Abraham and Moses because of Jesus

13 For I am speaking to you Gentiles. Inasmuch as I am the apostle to the

Gentiles, I magnify my ministry, 14 if somehow I may make my kinsmen jealous and may save some of them. 15 For if their rejection means the reconciliation of the world, what will their acceptance mean but life from the dead? 16 If the first portion of the dough is holy, the batch is also holy. And if the root is holy, so are the branches.

17 But if some of the branches were broken off, and you, being a wild olive shoot, were grafted in among them and became a partaker with them of the root and richness of the olive tree, 18 do not boast against the branches. If you boast, remember you do not sustain the root, but the root sustains you. 19 You will say then, "The branches were broken off, so that I might be grafted in." 20 This is correct. They were broken off because of unbelief, but you stand by faith. Do not be arrogant, but fear. 21 For if God did not spare the natural branches, neither will He spare you.

22 Therefore consider the goodness and severity of God—severity toward those who fell, but goodness toward you, if you continue in His goodness. Otherwise, you also will be cut off. 23 And these also, if they do not remain in unbelief, will be grafted in, for God is able to graft them in again. 24 For if you were cut out of the olive tree which is wild by nature, and were grafted contrary to nature into a cultivated olive tree, how much more will these, who are the natural branches, be grafted into their own olive tree?

3 HEALING

Chapter 3

Receiving and believing in Jesus Christ as your Saviour is the necessary. You must have faith to believe and receive the forgiveness of Jesus. Knowing that you have been forgiven and have communion with God releases joy in the human spirit that no words could describe. Knowing that as you pray that your prayers are received, and that God is with you and releasing angels to assist you brings comfort like nothing else ever could. If that was the only benefit to Jesus life, death, burial and resurrection, it would be worth rejoicing over throughout all of our human lives. However, Jesus not only redeemed us from sin but also the curse of it. Jesus also suffered horrible agony so that we may receive healing, health, and long life.

Isaiah 53: 5 But he was wounded for our transgressions,
   he was bruised for our iniquities;
the chastisement of our peace was upon him,
   and by his stripes we are healed.
6 All of us like sheep have gone astray;
   each of us has turned to his own way,
but the Lord has laid on him
   the iniquity of us all.

Faith in Jesus as Healer

By his stripes we are healed. By his suffering and the beatings he endured, he took them so that we may be healed. All of the sins of the world, all the suffering of the world m all the consequences of sin were placed upon Jesus who died on the cross. First, I explain that at any time Jesus could have resisted and called upon angels to rescue him. Jesus could have fought against his enemies because they were the enemies of God. He endured the suffering though on purpose so that he might also bear the punishment for sin by dying on the cross. He died. He rose from the dead being triumphant over all the power of the enemy. Because Jesus endured, His blood is applied to our lives if we will believe in him. Because Jesus is life, and there was no sin in him, death could not hold him.

Although many people believe Jesus died for them, they do not have the teaching that Jesus took the curse of sin so that we who believe in him can be healed. Throughout his earthly ministry, Jesus went about healing people. Through his death and resurrection, he commanded his disciples to heal the sick in the name of Jesus. That means it is God's expressed desire to heal. Jesus healed people because God desires his people to be healthy and strong and to enjoy their lives.

Hebrews 13: 8 Jesus Christ is the same yesterday, and today, and forever.

During Jesus ministry, a leper came to Jesus saying that he believed that if Jesus willed it or wanted it, He could heal him. Jesus expressed the will of God in his sentence to him.

Luke 5: 13 He reached out His hand and touched him, saying, "I will. Be clean." And immediately the leprosy left him.

God's will is health

It is God's desire to heal people because sickness, disease, pain are all a result of the curse of sin. In Deuteronomy God gives Moses both the blessings of following God's Word and the results of sinning against God. Sickness is part of the curse of sin. It was never supposed to be upon people. Because of Adam and Eve's sin, sickness, disease, suffering and death are the result.

Deuteronomy 28: 58 If you are not careful to observe all the words of this law that are written in this book so that you may fear this glorious and fearful name, the Lord your God, 59 then the Lord will bring extraordinary plagues on you and your descendants, even great long-lasting plagues, and severe and long-lasting sicknesses.

Living in covenant with God means health

God lists sickness and disease as part of the curse of sinning against God. Never believe the lie that God send a sickness to you to teach you something. God can teach you as long as you are living, but sickness is not a teaching tool God chooses. God clearly teaches it is the result of sin, a result of the curse of sin. God's people are to live long and healthy and believe God for health, fertility, strength and all types of comfort and provision. In Deuteronomy there is a listing of the blessings of serving God and a list of curses for sinning against God. In no place will you find that God uses sickness or disease to teach or to put upon his people. It is essential you get anchored in the truth that God wants you whole. SHALOM, used to greet each other in Hebrew means nothing missing; nothing broken. It means fullest possible excellence of peace. By studying what God desires for you by reading Deuteronomy, you will see it is repeatedly spoken that God desires to bless, to build up, to prosper his people.

Deuteronomy 28: 12 The Lord will open up to you His good treasure, the heavens, to give the rain to your land in its season and to bless all the work of your hand. You will lend to many nations, but you will not borrow. 13 The Lord will make you the head and not the tail; you will only be above and you will not be beneath, if you listen to the commandments of the Lord your God, which I am commanding you today, to observe and to do them. 14 Also, you shall not turn aside from any of the words which I am commanding you today, to the right hand or to the left, to go after other gods to serve them.

Long Life

Once you realize the truth of God's Word that just as sin is not God's will for you, neither is sickness, you can start to build your faith to receive your healing. You must first see the goodness of God that He blesses his children with health and long life.

Psalm 91: 16 With long life I will satisfy him
and show him My salvation.

Moses lived to be 120 years old. The day he died, God told him to climb to the top of a mountain so that he could die. He had to be pretty strong to climb the mountain. You do not have to die from sickness or disease. You can live your life fully enjoying it until the last day. Your transition to the next life can be as painless as slipping one garment off and slipping another one on. You will shed your earthly body, be clothed in your resurrection body and ascend to be with God. Those of us who are living on the earth when the Rapture of the church occurs, all people who are Christians will be transformed in the twinkling of an eye or in a fraction of a moment; we will be transformed with spiritual bodies that will never die.

Sickness is of the curse of sin

If sickness or disease tries to come upon you, you can resist it in the name of Jesus. Just as you can resist sin, you can resist the curse of sin. It isn't mental ascent. It isn't human will power. It requires faith. Faith is the spiritual substance that releases our will to believe God. Faith is believing

God's Word and praying it, confessing it and aligning your life with God's Word. Faith is evidence or proof of believing God. You can not do anything in the spirit realm without faith. Faith was required for you to receive your salvation. Faith is required to receive anything from God.

Hebrews 11: 1 Now faith is the substance of things hoped for, the evidence of things not seen. 2 For by it the men of old obtained a good report.

Hebrews 11: 6 And without faith it is impossible to please God, for he who comes to God must believe that He exists and that He is a rewarder of those who diligently seek Him.

Since faith is so important, it is very important that you strengthen your faith. Every person is given a measure of faith (Romans 12: 3). So there is potential in all people to have faith. Faith comes only one way: by hearing God's Word.

Romans 10: 16 But they have not all obeyed the gospel. For Isaiah says, "Lord, who has believed our report?"[h] 17 So then faith comes by hearing, and hearing by the word of God.

Faith comes by hearing God's word. It can be preaching; it can be teaching; it can be your own mouth praying scripture; it can be through CD's or DVD's. You can build or strengthen your faith so that you can receive faith for healing. It is not you. Don't say to yourself, I don't have that kind of faith. You can get it. No one would have faith for healing if he or she didn't strengthen his or her faith.

The way

Get preaching or teaching on healing. If you could get into a meeting where healing is being preached from the pulpit, get into those meetings. In some churches I have been a part of, it was normal for us to pray for healing regularly. There were constant testimonies of God healing people. Often the preacher preaches the word and people are healed spontaneously without someone laying hands on them. Faith can arise in your heart from hearing the word preached.

Faith can come by responding to an altar call for healing. Regularly the church should pray for healing for people. It means by faith in the scriptures they are obeying God's Word so God's people can be made whole.

James 5: 14 Is anyone sick among you? Let him call for the elders of the church, and let them pray over him, anointing him with oil in the name of the Lord. 15 And the prayer of faith will save the sick, and the Lord will raise him up. And if he has committed any sins, he will be forgiven.

Receive the healing by prayer

You may not feel 100 strong in your own faith, but if tow or more gather in Jesus name, it shall be done for them what they ask. An elder or minister of God will join his or her faith with yours believing that God will keep His Word. You may be healed in that way. It could be immediate. It could be progressive. It could be gradual. Should I require it, I would be persistent and try a varied approach.

Scriptures: pray God's Word

Search the scriptures and find scriptures on healing. I didn't know this was a scriptural way of prayer until I needed it desperately. My pastor, was deathly ill. I started praying. I praying in English; I prayed in tongues. I knew within my spirit it was not God's will for him to die. I knew the only way was for me to pray and keep praying. I'm sure the other people praying have their own testimonies about why we prayed and kept praying, but I am giving you mine. I searched the Strong's concordance (no Internet in those days) and found every possible scripture that had to do with healing. I started praying each scripture over my pastor as though it was for him specifically. There were many scriptures. I wrote them out on pages and would pray them each day. If you have not done this thing, begin to do it. Things are much easier with the Internet now, you can do a search and get results of hundreds of scriptures with the click of your mouse.

1. Search the scriptures for your topic or situation.
2. Write or print them for yourself and keep them near you. At least once a day pray over yourself those scriptures. Claim them as scriptures for your own life. Speak them over your body so that healing might flow through your physical body.
3. Begin to confess those scriptures as your words applying to your life. Speak by faith what God's word says.
4. Receive by faith your healing. Take it as though you know that it is God's gift to you.
5. Get into meetings where people preach and teach the scriptures with faith.
6. Should there be a service for healing or meetings for a healing

Evangelist, get into them. Get as much Word in you as possible.
7.   It may mean you watch little or no television except for that which builds you up in your faith. It many mean you give no place to people who doubt God in your life during that period. Receiving your healing is as important as knowing the scriptures. Receiving is an action. Just as I throw a ball to you and you catch it in your glove, receiving healing is grabbing on to it in the spirit. Praise God and thank God for what He has given you. Tell others about the goodness of God by giving your testimony. Some people publish it in books or magazines or even the newspaper. The more you share about what God has done for you, the more others will be inspired to believe for themselves. It wouldn't be right to receive a healing or miracle from God and not to share what God has done for you. Give God all the glory.

The scriptures give all sorts of different types of healing, By seeing the different kinds of healing, you faith can be built up and strengthened. You should start building up your faith now so your faith will be strong should occasion rise against you.

Jesus healed them all.

The scripture shows that on some occasions faith was strong in the people and Jesus healed them all.

Matthew 12: 15 But when Jesus knew it, He withdrew from there. And great crowds followed Him, and He healed them all, 16 and warned them that they should not make Him known, 17 to fulfill what was spoken by Isaiah the prophet, saying:

18 "Here is My Servant, whom I have chosen,
    My Beloved, in whom My soul is well pleased;
I will put My Spirit upon Him,
    and He will render judgment to the Gentiles.
19 He shall not struggle nor cry out,
    nor will anyone hear His voice in the streets.
20 A bruised reed He will not break,
    and a smoldering wick He will not quench,
until He renders judgment unto victory;
21   and in His name will the Gentiles trust."[a]

Jesus healed many

In some instances, in scripture, the phrase is used that Jesus healed many. It is not that Jesus wasn't willing to release his faith for healing, but there was no receiver in all instances. It takes faith to receive a healing or miracle. It can be your faith, or someone else's faith but there must be faith to receive it.

Mark 1: 32 In the evening, when the sun had set, they brought to Him all who were sick and those who were possessed with demons. 33 The whole city was gathered at the door, 34 and He healed many who were sick with various diseases and cast out many demons. And He did not let the demons speak, because they knew Him.

Luke 4: 38 He went out of the synagogue and entered Simon's house. Now Simon's mother-in-law was taken ill with a high fever, and they asked Him about her. 39 So He stood over her and rebuked the fever, and it left her. And immediately she rose and served them.

40 Now when the sun was setting, all those who had anyone sick with various diseases brought them to Him. And He laid His hands on every one of them and healed them. 41 And demons came out of many, crying out, "You are the Christ, the Son of God!" But He rebuked them and did not permit them to speak, because they knew that He was the Christ.

Because of their unbelief Jesus could not heal

It is pretty horrible, but in some places Jesus preached and taught, Jesus couldn't heal because they would not receive because they did not believe. It's hard to conceive of and you might say surely Jesus faith wasn't weak. That is certainly true. Jesus' faith was strong. The power to heal was there. Jesus was there willing to heal but there was no receiver. Faith must also have a receiver. It could be a person or the person's friend or a relative. There must be someone expressing faith in God. If there is no faith, you cannot receive anything from God.

Mark 6: 4 Jesus said to them, "A prophet is not without honor, except in his own country, and among his own relatives, and in his own house." 5 He could not do any miracles there, except that He laid His hands on a few sick people and healed them. 6 And He was amazed because of their unbelief

Hebrews 11: 6 And without faith it is impossible to please God, for he who comes to God must believe that He exists and that He is a rewarder of those who diligently seek Him.

In Jesus hometown, the unbelief was so strong that Jesus did no healings or miracles.

In Nazareth. Unbelief is sin. Whatever is not of faith is sin (Romans 14: 23).

Matthew 13: But Jesus said to them, "A prophet is not without honor except in his own country and in his own house."

58 And He did not do many mighty works there because of their unbelief.

The Atmosphere

In some instances, the town was so full of unbelief, Jesus had to lead someone outside of the town for healing. In the example below there was a blind man who wanted healing. Jesus led him out of the town. Outside the town, he spit on his eyes for healing. He used this method more than once although I believe he would have obeyed the Holy Spirit's prompting to do whatever he should. Healings do not always occur the same ways for people. It is not a formula. It is faith and obedience to the Holy Spirit. The man's vision was less than perfect. He could see something but not clearly. Jesus gave him a second touch of healing and the man was healed completely. The faith of the community had something to do with the man receiving his healing.

Mark 8 : 22 He came to Bethsaida. And they brought a blind man to Him and entreated Him to touch him. 23 He took the blind man by the hand and led him out of the town. When He had spit on his eyes and put His hands on him, He asked him, "Do you see anything?"
24 He looked up and said, "I see men as trees, walking."
25 Then again He put His hands on his eyes and made him look up. And he was restored and saw everyone clearly. 26 He sent him home away to his house, saying, "Neither go into the town, nor tell it to anyone in the town."

An atmosphere for faith

Although it may seem harsh what I am saying but, you can't just let any old garbage roll on your tv screen or in your ears as music or in your home. You must provide your home to be a place of receiving from God. You must cut off things that do not directly build up your faith and strengthen you spiritually. It may mean you keep to yourself rather than listen to doubt, unbelief, fear, sin, foolishness. These things do not produce faith. There are also good things that are not sinful such as sports or comedies etc. If you require healing, you should focus on getting yourself an atmosphere that builds faith. It could be for a duration. For example, during the period I was praying for my pastor to be healed, I prayed every day before I went to school. After I completed my marking, I would pray again. I would go to prayer at church each night. It went on for a period of 2 years before my pastor was completely healed. It was as an assignment to me. I knew I wasn't stopping until he was free of his situation. I was only one of many.

Athletes training for competitions often do without certain foods in their diet during competition. They train longer. They forgo certain things with their goal in sight. It is focusing on the end result of you faith that should determine what you should do. It often includes temporary changes; Sometimes it gets you to make permanent changes because you realize the things you were doing were not faith builders and were really just casual habits such as watching tv for hours.

Getting serious

Getting serious about receiving from God is being willing to receive. God is willing; Jesus paid the penalty for our sins and the curse of them It is necessary to get the faith connection in your heart or the core of your being.

Sow and keep on sowing

I enjoy my garden and have for many years. Some vegetables only appearance and you harvest them during the season like tomatoes. Other things such as carrots can be harvested and then planted again because they've got a shorter growing season. To be sure you don't run out of carrots, plant some; wait, plant some more' as you reap them, plant again. Plant and keep on planting so that you may never run out of carrots. The same is true with God's word in you. Plant it into your heart by faith. Receive it by faith. Keep on planting the word of God in your life you will always have a crop of healing or whatever you are believing from God.

Ecclesiastes 11: 6 In the morning sow your seed,
    and in the evening do not let your hand rest;
because you do not know which activity will find success,
    this way or that way,
    or if the both will be good.

Sow the Word

The way to always have the Word of God to sow, is to keep it in your eyes, in your ears, in your mouth. Literally write it. Post it to your mirror or your visor in the car. Sow and keep on sowing by always being in the Word of God.

God instructed Moses who instructed Joshua who passed the truths on to all of Israel to keep God's Word as a priority so that they would live long and prosper.

Joshua 1: 6 "Be strong and courageous, for you shall provide the land that I swore to their fathers to give them as an inheritance for this people. 7 Be strong and very courageous, in order to act carefully in accordance with all the law that My servant Moses commanded you. Do not turn aside from it to the right or the left, so that you may succeed wherever you go. 8 This Book of the Law must not depart from your mouth. Meditate on it day and night so that you may act carefully according to all that is written in it. For then you will make your way successful, and you will be wise. 9 Have not I commanded you? Be strong and courageous. Do not be afraid or dismayed, for the Lord your God is with you wherever you go."

Jesus redeemed us so we might be saved, healed, delivered, blessed.

Galatians 3: 13 Christ has redeemed us from the curse of the law by being made a curse for us—as it is written, "Cursed is everyone who hangs on a tree"[f]— 14 so that the blessing of Abraham might come on the Gentiles through Jesus Christ, that we might receive the promise of the Spirit through faith.

Jesus healed people who were not Israelites

Jesus was speaking to a woman who was not an Israelite who begged healing for her daughter. Jesus spoke to her somewhat harshly comparing her to a dog rather than a covenant child. Her answer did not change. She begged even more even if her were to think of her as a dog.

Matthew 15: 21 Then Jesus went from there and departed into the regions of Tyre and Sidon. 22 There, a woman of Canaan came out of the same regions and cried out to Him, saying, "Have mercy on me, O Lord, Son of David. My daughter is severely possessed by a demon."

26 But He answered, "It is not fair to take the children's bread and to throw it to dogs." 27 She said, "Yes, Lord, yet even dogs eat the crumbs that fall from their masters' table."

Jesus granted her petition because of her faith. Jesus healed people who had faith even though they were not the children of Israel.

Matthew 15: 28 Then Jesus answered her, "O woman, great is your faith. Let it be done for you as you desire." And her daughter was healed instantly.

Jesus gave authority to his disciples to preach and heal in Jesus name. He gave them authority to preach to all people not just the Jews,

Luke 24: 44 He said to them, "These are the words which I spoke to you while I was still with you, that all things must be fulfilled which were written in the Law of Moses and in the Prophets and in the Psalms concerning Me."

45 Then He opened their minds to understand the Scriptures. 46 He said to them, "Thus it is written, and accordingly it was necessary for the Christ to suffer and to rise from the dead the third day, 47 and that repentance and remission of sins should be preached in His name to all nations, beginning at Jerusalem. 48 You are witnesses of these things. 49 And look, I am sending the promise of My Father upon you. But wait in the city of Jerusalem until you are clothed with power from on high."

Faith is a key ingredient to receive healing

It was the woman's faith

Your faith in Jesus can bring healing without any person praying for you. There was a woman who was hemorrhaging, bleeding for 12 years. She spent money on trying get get solutions and remedies but there was no answer for her. One day though she had heard about the mighty healer Jesus and believed within herself that if she could just touch the hem of his robe, she could be healed. She had faith. Her point of connection for her faith was touch his robe. She believed. Even though there was hundreds of people there all pressing against each other in a crowd, Jesus felt something different. He felt faith touch him and virtue go out from him. Literally she reached and touched in faith expecting to receive and received her healing all in one moment.

Mark 5: 32 And He looked around to see her who had done it. 33 But the woman, fearing and trembling, knowing what had happened to her, came and fell down before Him and told Him the entire truth. 34 He said to her, "Daughter, your faith has made you well. Go in peace, and be healed of your affliction."

Jesus will to heal – special presence of healing

There were certain instances where people's faith were not strong in themselves. A leper's faith was in Jesus. He thought if Jesus wanted to heal me he could. He spoke those words to Jesus. His point of faith contact was in Jesus willingness to do it. Jesus spoke "I will." Jesus met the man at his point f faith, because of it, the leper was healed.

Mark 1: 40 A leper came to Him, pleading with Him and kneeling before Him, saying, "If You are willing, You can make me clean."

41 Then Jesus, moved with compassion, extended His hand and touched him, and said to him, "I will. Be clean." 42 As soon as He had spoken, the leprosy immediately departed from him, and he was cleansed.
In a different passage the faith of the man's friends not in the man himself was the point of faith to receive healing. Jesus was speaking and the home was crowded. People gathered around him to listen to his words and if they needed healing. There was no room for the men who carried their paralyzed friend on a mat. They would not be deterred though and they climbed up on the roof and brought their friend to Jesus on the ground. They literally made a hole in the roof to do it.

The faith of the friends brought healing to their friend.

The friends believed if they could get their friend to Jesus, he would heal him. Jesus used the man to also preach forgiveness as well as healing. Jesus knew by the Holy Spirit that he had unrepented sin in his life. Jesus first spoke that his sins were forgiven. That got everyone's attention because only God can forgive sins. He was stating that He was God.

Mark 2: 3 They came to Him bringing one sick with paralysis, who was carried by four men. 4 When they could not come near Him due to the crowding, they uncovered the roof where He was. When they had broken it open, they let down the bed on which the paralytic lay. 5 When Jesus saw their faith, He said to the paralytic, "Son, your sins are forgiven you."

Jesus forgave and healed.

As the scribes and Pharisees murmured about what Jesus was saying, Jesus used it to illustrate his sermon. He immediately asks them which is easier to forgive sins or to bring healing to a paralyzed man. They could do neither. With his words he commanded the man to receive forgiveness of sins and healing simultaneously.

Mark 2: 6 But some of the scribes were sitting there, reasoning in their hearts, 7 "Why does this Man speak such blasphemies? Who can forgive sins but God alone?"

Mark 2: 8 Immediately, when Jesus perceived in His spirit that they so reasoned within themselves, He said to them, "Why do you contemplate these things in your hearts? 9 Which is easier to say to the paralytic: 'Your sins are forgiven you,' or to say, 'Rise, take up your bed and walk'? 10 But that you may know that the Son of Man has authority on earth to forgive sins," He said to the paralytic, 11 "I say to you, rise, and take up your bed, and go your way to your house." 12 Immediately he rose, picked up the bed, and went out in front of them all, so that they were all amazed and glorified God, saying, "We never saw anything like this!"

The man's friends believed and because of it, Jesus both healed the man spiritually and physically because of it.

Disciples healed

Later in the book of Acts, after the disciples had been baptized in the Holy Spirit, Peter and John were on their way to a prayer meeting when they saw a paralyzed man begging.

Faith of Peter and John imparted healing

Peter's point to reach the man was to say, I will give you what I have in the name of Jesus. The beggar looked towards him expecting to receive something and he did. He may have thought some money was coming his way but what did come is healing. Peter commanded him to rise up in the name of Jesus. The man stood and walked and jumped because he had received a miracle of healing. The Holy Spirit will often quicken people to pray for people for healing or to speak words to people so they may receive from God. Obedience to the Holy Spirit is essential to be used by God in any type of ministry.

Acts 3: 1 Now Peter and John went up together to the temple at the ninth hour, the hour of prayer. 2 A man lame from birth was being carried, whom people placed daily at the gate of the temple called Beautiful to ask alms from those who entered the temple. 3 Seeing Peter and John about to go into the temple, he asked for alms. 4 Peter, gazing at him with John, said, "Look at us." 5 So he paid attention to them, expecting to receive something from them.

6 Then Peter said, "I have no silver and gold, but I give you what I have. In the name of Jesus Christ of Nazareth, rise up and walk." 7 He took him by the right hand and raised him up. Immediately his feet and ankles were strengthened. 8 Jumping up, he stood and walked and entered the temple with them, walking and jumping and praising God. 9 All the people saw him walking and praising God. 10 They knew that it was he who sat for alms at the Beautiful Gate of the temple. And they were filled with wonder and amazement at what happened to him.

Healing is a blessing of covenant with God.

1. Search the scriptures for your topic or situation.
2. Write or print them for yourself and keep them near you. At least once a day pray over yourself those scriptures. Claim them as scriptures for your own life. Speak them over your body so that healing might flow through your physical body.
3. Begin to confess those scriptures as your words applying to your life. Speak by faith what God's word says.
4. Receive by faith your healing. Take it as though you know that it is God's gift to you.
5. Get into meetings where people preach and teach the scriptures with faith for healing.
6. Should there be a service for healing or meetings for a healing Evangelist, get into them. Get as much Word in you as possible.
7. Get an atmosphere for faith in your home. Cut out distractions. Cut off people who do not feed your faith. Cut off activities that do not build your faith.

Tell others about the goodness of God by giving your testimony. Some people publish it in books or magazines or even the newspaper. The more you share about what God has done for you, the more others will be inspired to believe for themselves. It wouldn't be right to receive a healing or miracle from God and not to share what God has done for you. Give God all the glory.

.

4 DELIVERANCE

Chapter 4

Deliverance means to be set free. It means freedom in all areas of life. People who do not know God could be in bondage in sin, iniquity or strongholds of addiction. Also, some Christians can be in bondage to these things also. This chapter will explain the root of addiction and show how Jesus cast out demons and set captives free.

Sin causes addiction.

Non-Christians still have free will. A demon cannot gain entrance into a person without that person yielding his or her will. Just as Adam and Eve, willingly took part of something God had forbidden, non-Christians must give up their will to be in bondage. A simple example would be getting drunk. If a person drinks alcohol with the desire to get drunk, the person is willfully sinning. Drinking alcohol is not a sin but getting drunk is. A person drunk or intoxicated with alcohol often experiences a loss of self-control. The person's body may be affected by it. The person's voice etc. will be affected. The alcohol or drugs or addiction substance is pleasurable and induces a type of alternate reality for the person.

Usually people who purposely drink to get drunk or stoned are trying to forget something or someone. It could be a relationship. It could be the loss of a loved one or some real negative aspect of the person's life he or she doesn't want to remember; the alcohol or drug releases the person from reality by the illusion of an alternate reality, The person believes the alternate state or "high" is preferable to regular life.

Iniquity is inherited sin from your family.

Iniquity is sin that has become a habit that becomes a life choice. It is a pattern of repeated sin; it can be passed on to other generations because it is a repeated sin against God. For instance, a person born into a family of alcohol or drug addiction, will likely also become addicted. It is genetically inherited as well as spiritually. Science shows the dna patterns to be similar and in the spiritual realm the same thing occurs. That is why for example there are families that are known as alcoholics or adulterers. The sin once repeatedly chosen over God's word becomes like a trench in the person's life causing that person to choose it repeatedly. The Bible refers to it as a conscience that is hardened. A person who is in iniquity may be oppressed by a demon. That means, as that person sins, a demon my use the person's body and soul. When people are yielding their will to sin, they leave part of their souls open to demonic influence.

A Christian can be oppressed by a demon if he or she is in willful sin. The demon may not possess the person but surely will oppress the person.

Oppression

Oppression is being bound or chained to a sin, hating the sin because you know it is wrong, but doing it anyway. It is yielding to sin. Afterwards the person will feel terrible remorse and repent. If there is a sin that habitually bothers you, it would be best to pray asking God to reveal the source. Sin cannot manifest without an entrance point. For instance, you might need to plead the blood of Jesus over your family heritage and cut off any ties to sinful things. It could be movies, music, jewelry. If it represents a different god or some other idolatry, it can be an entry point for sin in your home. The good news is you do not have to be bound to any sin. You can be set free by Jesus.

1 Thessalonians 4: 3 For this is the will of God, your sanctification: that you should abstain from sexual immorality, 4 that each one of you should know how to possess his own vessel in sanctification and honor, 5 not in the lust of depravity, even as the Gentiles who do not know God, 6 and that no man take advantage of and defraud his brother in any matter, because the Lord is the avenger in all these things, as we also have forewarned you and testified. 7 For God has not called us to uncleanness, but to holiness. 8 Therefore he that despises does not despise man, but God, who has also given us His Holy Spirit.

Ephesians 4: 17 Therefore this I say and testify in the Lord, that from now on you walk not as other Gentiles walk, in the vanity of their minds, 18 having their understanding darkened, excluded from the life of God through the ignorance that is within them, due to the hardness of their hearts. 19 Being calloused they have given themselves over to sensuality for the practice of every kind of impurity with greediness.

Strong holds

A stronghold means that a person has repeatedly sinned in an area in his or her conscience no longer shows; the person doesn't know it is a sin anymore. A person who willingly sins can become possessed by a demon. The person is yielding that part of his human spirit.

Possession

Possession occurs when a person continues to willfully sin and does not turn to God. A person with sin becomes ensnared in the sins and they multiply. First comes the bondage; next the person cannot get free. The person cannot help himself or herself because he or she has willfully given himself/herself over to the addictions. There are demons that can possess those parts of a person. It can cause the person to do things he or she would not normally do such as become violent or commit crimes, or take their own lives.

Luke 11: 24 "When an unclean spirit goes out of a man, it goes through dry places seeking rest. Finding none, it says, 'I will return to my house, from which I came.' 25 When it comes, it finds it swept and furnished. 26 Then it goes and brings seven other spirits more wicked than itself, and they enter and dwell there. And the last state of that man is worse than the first."

The good news is that even if a person were possessed by a demon, the person can be set free. It must be the person's human will that chooses though. A person who recognizes that he or she is doing things that are against God's Word and usually also against the law, may have a moment of realizing he or she doesn't want to do it. That moment is a moment of God's mercy towards that person. It is as though there is a space where God's mercy can come in and the person can be set free. For instance, people who want to be set free, seek exorcism or the casting out of demons.

2 Corinthians 10: 3 For though we walk in the flesh, we do not war according to the flesh. 4 For the weapons of our warfare are not carnal, but mighty through God to the pulling down of strongholds, 5 casting down imaginations and every high thing that exalts itself against the knowledge of God, bringing every thought into captivity to the obedience of Christ, 6 and being ready to punish all disobedience when your obedience is complete.

If you or a loved one is bound in sin and addiction, you can be set free. If you or a loved one are possessed by a demon, you can be set free. It must begin with you. You must decide if you want to be set free. It seems like there would be no question you would want to be set free. However, there is some pleasurable aspect to the sin that keeps a person in bondage.

For instance, many people like the feeling of an alternate reality that is induced by alcohol or drugs. You must renounce the sin to be free.

Exorcism or casting out demons

Only an experienced believer should partake in exorcism or casting out of demons. Usually a person does not do it alone. Usually there are people who are praying while it is occurring. It is Justas real as having someone come and place a shelter on your property and start living there while you own it. It is called squatter's rights. If you let that person live in that space long enough, the person can claim it as his own. The same is true of demons and people. The demons will only possess someone who does not evict them. If a person is not strong in his or her own faith he should get a mature, strong Christian to do it. The example shows how for instance the sons of Sceva tried to copy the apostle Paul, without knowing God as did Apostle Paul. They were abused and wounded by the experience.

Acts 19: 13 Then some of the itinerant Jewish exorcists invoked the name of the Lord Jesus over those who had evil spirits, saying, "We command you to come out in the name of Jesus whom Paul preaches." 14 There were seven sons of a Jewish high priest named Sceva doing this. 15 The evil spirit answered, "I know Jesus, and I know Paul, but who are you?" 16 Then the man in whom the evil spirit was jumped on them, overpowered them, and prevailed against them, so that they fled from that house naked and wounded.

IMPORTANT

First to undergird your faith or build up your faith for the topic, I will examine how Jesus fulfilled the prophecy to do it. Later I will give you examples of how Jesus cast out evil spirits; finally, I will discuss deliverance and what to do to get it.

In the scripture about the Messiah, the Messiah is stricken or beaten and whipped. He was wounded for our sins. That means because he was wounded, we can be set free. It means because he was abused, in his body and in his soul, we can be healed. The chastisement of our peace was upon him means that in all matters regarding human peace, Jesus is Lord. If there is anything in life that would try to steal your peace to cause you want to escape reality, Jesus can heal you so you will enjoy life. Jesus can heal you in your soul from anything that you have lived through. God wants you to enjoy your life. God wants you to be joyful. You can be so secure in your relationship with God that you are unshakable.

Jesus the Messiah fulfilled the scriptures. He is our peace.

Is 53: 1 Surely, he has borne our grief
 and carried our sorrows;
Yet we esteemed him stricken,
 smitten of God, and afflicted.
5 But he was wounded for our transgressions,
 he was bruised for our iniquities;
the chastisement of our peace was upon him,
 and by his stripes we are healed.
6 All of us like sheep have gone astray;
 each of us has turned to his own way,
but the Lord has laid on him
 the iniquity of us all.

Jesus is our peace

Jesus is the prince of peace. He gives us perfect peace so that we are not tossed about like things in a storm. Jesus is our peace. His holy presence abiding in you gives you peace. Jesus promised us peace. He promised the Holy Spirit would come so that we would always have God's comfort with us.

John 14: 27 Peace I leave with you. My peace I give to you. Not as the world gives do I give to you. Let not your heart be troubled, neither let it be afraid.

Ephesians 2: 14 For He is our peace, who has made both groups one and has broken down the barrier of the dividing wall, 15 by abolishing in His flesh the enmity, that is, the law of the commandments contained in ordinances, that in Himself He might make the two into one new man, thus making peace, 16 and that He might reconcile both to God into one body through the cross, thereby slaying the enmity. 17 And He came and preached peace to you who were far away and peace to those who were near. 18 For through Him we both have access by one Spirit to the Father.

The anointing of God was on Jesus to proclaim liberty to the captives. Jesus preached the good news of eternal life. Jesus healed people physically and also in their soul – inner healing.

Jesus can heal a broken heart, There are people who lose a loved one and die of a broken heart. Literally it affects their soul so much, it causes them to not want to live and their inner self begins to die. Jesus can heal those people and repurpose their lives. Jesus came to set the captives free. People who are captives to sin and the power of sin can be set free. God can give a person beauty for ashes. Literally, some people have a tough life, without loving parents or family and they are wounded, used and abused. They have many reasons to stay an addict to things all their lives. They do not have to live that way though. They can be set free.

If you have not read Joyce Meyer's testimony or heard her tell it, I highly recommend to you that you get a copy. She knows what it is like to grow up in a totally abusive home and have a poor start in life. But God radically transformed her life through Jesus Christ. The transformation is not a simple one moment solution, but it begins with a moment. A person makes a decision to yield to God and let God heal him or her. One moment can make all the difference should you decide to choose Jesus.

God can give you life beyond what you have ever known in your best most awesome imagination. God can transform you so that you are not sin-conscience or needy and self-absorbed. God can set you free, so you can live free from anything you experienced in your past. Your past does not determine your future. You have a human will in the present. You can choose a different way. Choose God's way and He will set you free so that you can experience joy and abundance beyond what you could have ever known on your own.

Is 61: 1 The Spirit of the Lord God is upon me
   because the Lord has anointed me
   to preach good news to the poor;
He has sent me to heal the broken-hearted,
   to proclaim liberty to the captives,
   and the opening of the prison to those who are bound;
2 to proclaim the acceptable year of the Lord
   and the day of vengeance of our God;
to comfort all who mourn,
3   to preserve those who mourn in Zion,
to give to them beauty
   for ashes,
the oil of joy
   for mourning,
the garment of praise
   for the spirit of heaviness,

that they might be called trees of righteousness,
    the planting of the Lord,
    that He might be glorified.

Please see the wording – beauty for ashes. I've been with people who have lost everything whether it be a loved one or a job or a home etc. I have seen people who believe that there is no future hope. That is the biggest lie that gets people to commit suicide. A person who believes there is no hope is in a terrible position. Our hope should be in Jesus Christ. Jesus living in us gives us more than enough of Himself in us and through us so that there is always hope. Someone who knows God, knows that Jesus is more than able to keep him or her through anything.

A person may only have ashes of life – really nothing to offer Jesus. Jesus though can give that same person beauty. The person chooses Jesus Christ. Jesus lives on the inside of the person and through the person. The person is renewed in his or her thinking and his or her habits and soon the person is completely transformed by God. God gives them beauty in all kinds of blessings in different areas of his or her life so that the person can truly say that God has transformed him or her.

Romans 12: 1 I urge you therefore, brothers, by the mercies of God, that you present your bodies as a living sacrifice, holy, and acceptable to God, which is your reasonable service of worship. 2 Do not be conformed to this world, but be transformed by the renewing of your mind, that you may prove what is the good and acceptable and perfect will of God.

Often a person who believes his or her life is in ashes or with nothing or of no value, can be transformed by God to be a person who values his or her life and becomes a giver and an encourager to others. The exact opposite of nothing. The person will begin to care about others and not only know his or her own worth to God but also encourage, built up and strengthen others.

Being Set Free

Often a person who has been possessed or oppressed by demons will lose a chunk of their lives as it is cast out. The person who is possessed or oppressed by a demon, thinks about the addiction, spends all of his or her life getting that addiction at any cost. The person may break the law to get the addiction. The person will partake of the addiction but will never be satisfied. The person will always return to it. The scripture phrases it as such.

Proverbs 26: 11 As a dog returns to its vomit,
   so a fool returns to his folly.

2 Peter 2: 22 But it has happened to them according to the true proverb, "The dog returns to his own vomit,"[a] and "the sow that was washed to her wallowing in the mud."

Freedom

    The person's thoughts, words, actions, habits, days and life are spent in the addiction. It is a huge part of his or her life. What must occur is that something must replace those parts of a person's life if he or she is to be free and stay free. First is recognizing that you were bound by sin and addiction. If a person cannot recognize the truth, he or she cannot be changed. A person who undergoes deliverance must make a commitment to Jesus. I would highly recommend the person attend classes on staying free of addictions at church. There are many such classes available. The core tenants of the class are acknowledging you need to make life changes in choices to stay free.

    The purpose of my book is not to in depth discuss methods, and practice but to let you know that there is an answer for you and its more awesome than you could ever imagine.

John 8: 32 You shall know the truth, and the truth shall set you free."

John 14: 6 Jesus said to him, "I am the way, the truth, and the life. No one comes to the Father except through Me. 7 If you had known Me, you would have known My Father also. From now on you do know Him and have seen Him."

8 Philip said to Him, "Lord, show us the Father, and that is sufficient for us."

John 10: 10 The thief does not come, except to steal and kill and destroy. I came that they may have life, and that they may have it more abundantly.

Jesus is the life; Jesus came to give us abundant life; Jesus can resurrect your life so that it is more exciting and joyful than you could ever have imagined.

Jesus cast out demons throughout his earthly ministry. Sin begins an addiction. It starts with doing something the person knows is wrong but does anyway.

A person who sins is willfully breaking God's commandments. With Jesus Christ's Holy Spirit on the inside of you, you will know it. You will either repent or continue to do it. Each person makes a personal choice of human will. God hates sin because of what it does to people. Sin destroys people's lives. For instance, drinking alcohol is not wrong, but a person drinking bottle after bottle of alcohol addicted to it affects all the people in his life. It may mean that children have no caring parents, or the person may get a divorce because his or her partner cannot live with the addiction. Sin separates people from God; sin separates people from loved ones.

1 John 3: 8 Whoever practices sin is of the devil, for the devil has been sinning from the beginning. For this purpose, the Son of God was revealed, that He might destroy the works of the devil. 9 Whoever has been born of God does not practice sin, for His seed remains in him. And he cannot keep on sinning, because he has been born of God.

The Healing of the Gergesene Demoniacs

There is no mention in the Old Testament Scriptures of demons being cast out. Jesus could do it because he was the Messiah. Adam and Eve's sin and sin consciousness were not in Jesus. Jesus was holy; he could cast out demons because they had no part in him. As Jesus approached the country of the Gergesene in the scripture had demons manifesting in people they possessed. The reason the demons manifested is because Jesus was God. Jesus was able to cast them out. When I say manifest, demons are not constantly manifesting in a person. They do it sporadically. Often, they do not manifest because they do not want to be cast out. It is as though a person has stolen a vehicle and is using that vehicle to drive around. The person may not want to drive around in busy traffic because he knows the license plate could lead to his detection and arrest.

The demons possessing the person cried out. They knew it was not yet judgement day and that demons will be judged on judgement day. The demons realized that since Jesus saw them he could cast them out. Jesus cast them into the herd of swine. The demons possessed the pigs and ran them off the cliff. Demons destroy. The death of the pigs is not the end of the demons. They will search for a new place to live.

Matthew 8: 28 When He came to the other side into the country of the Gergesenes, there met Him two men possessed with demons, coming out of the tombs, extremely fierce, so that no one might pass by that way. 29 Suddenly they cried out, saying, "What have we to do with You, Jesus, Son of God? Have You come here to torment us before the time?"

30 Now a good way off from them was a herd of many swine feeding. 31 So the demons begged Him, saying, "If You cast us out, permit us to go away into the herd of swine."

32 He said to them, "Go!" And when they came out, they went into the herd of swine. And suddenly the whole herd of swine ran violently down a steep place into the sea, and perished in the waters. 33 Those who kept them fled, and went their ways into the city, and told everything, including what had happened to those possessed by the demons. 34 The whole city came out to meet Jesus. And when they saw Him, they begged Him to depart out of their region.

Jesus cast out demons

We know that Mary Magdalene, who was once a harlot had demons cast out of her. her life was completely changed. She became a devout follower of Jesus. She was present as he died on the cross. She was the first person to the tomb on the day of his resurrection. Her life was radically transformed so that she lived following Jesus.

Mark 16: 9 Now when Jesus rose early on the first day of the week, He appeared first to Mary Magdalene, out of whom He had cast seven demons. 10 She went and told those who had been with Him as they mourned and wept. 11 When they heard that He was alive and had been seen by her, they did not believe it.

By Jesus death, burial and descending into Sheol/Hades, and Abraham's Bosom, the place the dead were once kept, he defeated Satan completely. Jesus not only defeated Satan it says he made an open show of him. This means that Jesus wasn't in a fighting match with someone equal. Jesus was as a huge superhero while the enemy was as a weakling. Jesus won the victory not only for himself but for all people who would believe in him. That means no demon can fight against Jesus – Jesus already defeated them. Jesus purchased the right for us to be free paying the full cost of his life for our lives so we could be set free.

Colossians 2: 13 And you, being dead in your sins and the uncircumcision of your flesh, He has resurrected together with Him, having forgiven you all sins. 14 He blotted out the handwriting of ordinances that was against us and contrary to us, and He took it out of the way, nailing it to the cross. 15 And having disarmed authorities and powers, He made a show of them openly, triumphing over them by the cross.

Jesus commissioned disciples to cast out demons

Even before Jesus died, he had authority over demons because Jesus is God. He can command them because they are creatures and He is the creator. Jesus gave authority to his disciples to cast out demons. Part of what it means to be a Christian means that we give our lives to preaching the good news of salivation, the healing of Jesus and casting out demons.

Matthew 10: 5 These twelve Jesus sent out, and commanded them, saying, "Do not go into the way of the Gentiles, and do not enter any city of the Samaritans. 6 But go rather to the lost sheep of the house of Israel. 7 As you go, preach, saying, 'The kingdom of heaven is at hand.' 8 Heal the sick, cleanse the lepers, raise the dead, and cast out demons. Freely you have received, freely give.

There is an instance with the Apostle Paul who knows that a girl following him is possessed by an evil spirit. It was not her words. She sounded like she was praising God. She was announcing that the they were servants of the highest God. In reality, the demon was mocking God. The apostle Paul did nothing for several days, finally he discerned it was an evil spirit and he cast it out of her. No longer could she do the magic and things she did while she was demon possessed. Because of it, her master got very angry as he had lost a good source of income from the girl's magical gifts.

Acts 16: 16 On one occasion, as we went to the place of prayer, a servant girl possessed with a spirit of divination met us, who brought her masters much profit by fortune-telling. 17 She followed Paul and us, shouting, "These men are servants of the Most High God, who proclaim to us the way of salvation." 18 She did this for many days. But becoming greatly troubled, Paul turned to the spirit and said, "I command you in the name of Jesus Christ to come out of her." And it came out at that moment.

Jesus is the answer to any addictions or bondages; you may need to go to a different church or to a special service. Get into a meeting where deliverance is taught and preached and practiced. By hearing the truth, you can receive it and be set free.

Jesus brings life

Jesus plan for people is that we could have eternal peace with God beginning at the moment of salvation. It's comforting to know that as a Christian you will live with God forever, but it is life changing to know that you can start enjoying your life the moment you become a Christian. God's plan is for us to have abundant life, joyful life, peace and prosperity.

1 John 5: 10 Whoever believes in the Son of God has this witness in himself. Whoever does not believe God has made Him out to be a liar, because he does not believe the testimony that God gave about His Son. 11 And this is the testimony: that God has given us eternal life, and this life is in His Son. 12 Whoever has the Son has life, and whoever does not have the Son of God does not have life.

Deuteronomy 11: 21 so that your days and the days of your children may be multiplied in the land which the Lord swore to your fathers to give them, as long as the days of heaven on the earth.

Jesus sets you free

You can be set free whether it is demon possession, demon oppression or simply bad habits and occasion sins. You can be completely free from the desire of the sin. You can be transformed in your life so you enjoy your life rather than live in addiction.

John 8: 31 Then Jesus said to those Jews who believed Him, "If you remain in My word, then you are truly My disciples. 32 You shall know the truth, and the truth shall set you free."

33 They answered Him, "We are Abraham's seed and have never been in bondage to anyone. Why do You say, 'You shall be set free'? "

34 Jesus answered them, "Truly, truly I say to you, whoever commits sin is a slave of sin. 35 Now a slave does not remain in the house forever, but a son remains forever. 36 Therefore if the Son sets you free, you shall be free indeed.

John 10: 10 The thief does not come, except to steal and kill and destroy. I came that they may have life, and that they may have it more abundantly.

Give yourself wholly

First you must give yourself wholly to God. You are a spirit being. You have a soul (mind, will and emotions) and you live in a physical body. Your human will influences your spirit, your soul and your body. You must wholly give yourself to God. Accept Jesus as the Saviour that made peace with God for you, so your spirit may be quickened; receive Jesus healing and life in your soul so you can be set free in your mind, will and emotions. Receiving Jesus means the Holy Spirit comes to live inside of you. Your body is governed by your choices.

A Christian should be living in the spirit, with the spirit leading by the prompting of the Holy Spirit. A person who does not know Christ lives in his or her soul (mind will and emotions). Soulish life is concerned only about "me". The soul thinks about itself; does want it wants to do; does what it feels like doing. If you have not seen Joyce Meyer doing "the robot", please go to utube and watch one of the episodes. It is really funny but also so true. The soul not lead by the spirit is fleshly and carnal and self-absorbed.

Wholly

1 Thessalonians 5: 23 May the very God of peace sanctify you completely. And I pray to God that your whole spirit, soul, and body be preserved blameless unto the coming of our Lord Jesus Christ. 24 Faithful is He who calls you, who also will do it.

Once you've made the commitment to God with all your being, you must begin to get God's Word in you as much as possible, in as many ways as possible. I highly recommend doing it by attending a church class on living free from addictions. Such a class can help you to get excellent specific teaching to particular addictions and how to be free from them. It will connect you with new Christian friends who live differently than you have. You will be able to learn from them what a normal Christian life should be like. You will also get friendships that will last because you believe the same thing. It is the best way to do it in a church with believers.

Let God's Word transform you

Getting God's Word in you is essential. God's Word is His will for people. God's Word has within itself the power to bring itself to come to pass. God's Word releases faith so that you can be transformed by God's word. It has the power to change your soul. Getting the Word will mean getting into services that preach God's Word with faith.

Romans 12: 1 I urge you therefore, brothers, by the mercies of God, that you present your bodies as a living sacrifice, holy, and acceptable to God, which is your reasonable service of worship. 2 Do not be conformed to this world, but be transformed by the renewing of your mind, that you may prove what is the good and acceptable and perfect will of God.

James 1: 21 Therefore lay aside all filthiness and remaining wickedness and receive with meekness the engrafted word, which is able to save your souls.

Begin transformation with God's Word

Devotion

Get God's Word by reading the scripture each day. Choose at least 30 minutes to start with. Use it to pray, praise and read scripture. Remember to ask the Holy Spirit to quicken the scriptures to you. For a new believer or someone who has been set free, 30 minutes may seem long. If necessary, use a timer. Talk to God as you would to your most intimate friend. Ask God to teach you and show you how to live. Ask God to quicken the scriptures to you until you have them engrafted into your soul. Pray that God's Word would be so much in you that it would be as though you are a living epistle. That means you live the scripture rather than just know it.

Church services

Get into a Church that preaches with faith salvation, healing and deliverance. The worship should excite you. there should be healings and salvations and people using the gifts of the Holy Spirit in the Church. If those things are present, you are in the right place. Learn all you can. Take notes from the sermons. Worship wholly. Sign up for different types of adult classes so you can get deeper teaching and make friends. Volunteer to help with small things such as parking duty or ushering. You can do something. Do it with all your might to the excellence of God.

Christian Media

If your family are not Christians, you may not have anyone close to talk about spiritual things. Christian Media has made a big impact on my life because it has joined me with millions of believers all over the world. For instance Glory star is a Christian Satellite that has more than 30 Christian stations on it. You can get preaching, teaching, praise and worship, Christian movies and entertainment, Christian news. You can be joined with people who believe the same through Christian Media. I know myself it has been a true source of teaching me about God and letting me know what is going on in the Church of North America particularly. There are Christian radio stations, Christian music apps for your phone. There is a vast number of types of media choices available to you showing Jesus Christ as LORD.

Christian books

Christian books can be an excellent way to build yourself up on a particular topic especially if you can't get to see the evangelist or author speak in person. Books usually deal with one topic and in detail give scriptures supporting it. Invest in yourself so that you've got some resources to help you.

Christian friends

Some classes that help someone stay free from addictions often have people who will talk with you. You will also meet friends. Being able to talk to someone about something so important to your life is essential. Often people who were addicts did not have communication with anyone and were not good communicators. Getting true Christian friends is essential.

Your old addict friends won't want you in their lives if you keep talking about Jesus. They will not be encouraging you to live for God. The people who are addicts will not like you anymore because of your choice to be free. You will no longer like them because you will see how their addictions rule them and their life choices.

A good way to make Christian friends is by attending different kinds of Sunday school classes. Also, volunteering at Church helps you to meet other Christians. Often God will give you the right person in your life should you pray for Christian friends.

You are free

In an instance where Jesus was preaching in a synagogue on the Sabbath day, he was a woman who was bound in affliction. He spoke a word of healing to her that set her free. Jesus explains she was bound by a demon, because she is a daughter of Israel it is right to set her free evnoon the sabbath day. God's Holy Spirit can directly speak to your human spirit and you may receive total liberty or freedom from addiction or bondage. It can be in an instant. Usually though, God uses people to help you maintain your freedom in Christ after you have been delivered.

Luke 13: 10 He was teaching in one of the synagogues on the Sabbath. 11 And there was a woman who had a spirit of infirmity for eighteen years and was bent over and could not straighten herself up. 12 When Jesus saw her, He called her and said to her, "Woman, you are loosed from your infirmity." 13 Then He laid His hands on her, and immediately she was made straight and glorified God.

Unbind him

Part of what most occur is an unbinding. Should you unwrap a chord or a hose, you will occasionally get snags in it and need to do untangle it. In the same way, as your life is being transformed, God will place certain people in your life who will help you. The people will feel drawn to you. You will feel drawn to them There will be mutual benefit. They will share things with you helping you to grow in the Christian faith. You may help them in some way whether it be manual labour or some specific thing.

Proverbs 27: 17 Iron sharpens iron,
   so a man sharpens the countenance of his friend.

Jesus raised Lazarus from the dead

Jesus can resurrect your life after addiction, but often he uses people to unbind you. Being set free is much like a resurrection because all things are new. You must learn a new way of living. You will enjoy freedoms you never knew before. As in the example of Jesus raising Lazarus from the dead, your life can be raised in a new way so that you make wise choices and learn other ways of doing things. Jesus commanded the people to roll away the stone. He commanded Lazarus to come out of the tomb and out of death. Lazarus came hopping out of the grave. Jesus spoke to the disciples to release him or unbind him because he was still wrapped in his grave clothes.

John 11: 38 Then Jesus, again groaning within Himself, came to the tomb. It was a cave, and a stone was lying against it. 39 Jesus said, "Take away the stone."

Martha, the sister of him who was dead, said to Him, "Lord, by this time there is a stench, for he has been dead four days."

40 Jesus said to her, "Did I not tell you that if you believed, you would see the glory of God?"

41 So they took away the stone from the place where the dead man was lying. Jesus lifted up His eyes and said, "Father, I thank You that You have heard Me. 42 I know that You always hear Me. But because of the people standing around, I said this, that they may believe that You sent Me."

43 When He had said this, He cried out with a loud voice, "Lazarus, come out!" 44 He who was dead came out, his hands and feet wrapped with grave clothes, and his face wrapped with a cloth.

Jesus said to them, "Unbind him, and let him go."

In the same way that Jesus had others help Lazarus, He will place people in your life who can help you. An example would be mature Christian leaders who would mentor you in the things of faith. Also, there will be Christian friends who you can share experiences with such as concerts, movies etc.

After you have been set free, live in the freedom. You do that by giving no place to the enemy. It means you keep God's Word in your eyes and in your mouth and in your ears. It means getting the Word of God on the inside of you. It's not just listening; it is coming into spiritual alignment with God's Word.

The Word of God must be in your spirit, your mouth, your eyes etc. Word of God is a lamp it enlightens the way, it gives understanding it is wisdom from above.

Psalm 119: 105 Your word is a lamp for my feet,
    a light on my path.

Deuteronomy 11: 18 Fix these words of mine in your hearts and minds; tie them as symbols on your hands and bind them on your foreheads. 19 Teach them to your children, talking about them when you sit at home and when you walk along the road, when you lie down and when you get up. 20 Write them on the doorframes of your houses and on your gates, 21 so that your days and the days of your children may be many in the land the Lord swore to give your ancestors, as many as the days that the heavens are above the earth.

If you give yourself wholly to God and constantly receive the Word of God into your life and in your human spirit, you will be transformed. You will magnify God with your life. Rather than be focused on self-absorption, you will care for others and how you can give, serve and encourage others. Your freedom will so bring joy to you that you will want to evangelize sharing the truth with as many people as possible.

1.   Get into teaching or preaching of God's word with faith in salvation, healing and deliverance.
2.   Get involved in your church in volunteering.
3.   Get into Bible classes to learn all you can about God's word.
4.   Give God yourself each day, expecting God to use you to encourage others.
5. Be accountable to strong, mature Christian friends who will pray with you and help you in the faith.

5 LIVING IN THE ABUNDANCE
OF GOD'S BLESSING

Chapter 5

If you were not raised in a Christian home, or you have not been living for God and have returned to serve Him, you may need a reminder that it is God's will to bless you and prosper you. Many religious people do not know how good God is because they have not read or studied the scriptures. Also, they may believe lies or religious traditions rather than what the scriptures say.

I was not raised in a Christian home. I did not know the goodness of God. Throughout my life as a Christian, I have been discovering that He is more awesome than I could have imagined. He delights in giving you the desires of your heart. Just as a parent gives a toy or a present to his or her child with the point of desiring to see the child joyful, God is the same way with His people.

Luke 12: 32 "Do not be afraid, little flock, for your Father has been pleased to give you the kingdom.

Mark 11: 24 Therefore I tell you, whatever you ask for in prayer, believe that you have received it, and it will be yours.

Psalm 37: 4 Take delight in the Lord,
   and he will give you the desires of your heart.

The blessing of the Lord

Yes, it is true God wants you to have whatever you desire, as long as what you desire is within His will. That isn't a catch. If you are truly a Christian, you will not want to sin. You will want the best for your life. Sinful things always result in death. Just as with Adam and Eve and the fruit that was forbidden lead to their spiritual death, sin of any kind separates you from God. That is a horrible curse even if there was nothing else. Sin also has consequences. There is always death and negative consequences to disobedience to God.

Romans 6: 23 For the wages of sin is death, but the gift of God is eternal life in[b] Christ Jesus our Lord.

God's Will

You will know what is in God's will for you by reading God's Word. The commandments given to Moses are an excellent place to start. I do not mean that you should focus on keeping them with all your energy. Know the commandments. Get close to God by praying that the commandments are written on your heart. Pray that God can cause you to love what He loves and hate what He hates.

Getting the Word of God into you

Reading God's Word is essential. Get a translation you understand and enjoy. Read it every day. Create a space in your life for God. Literally book a duration of your day to spend reading the Bible and praying. It is excellent because you will begin to understand God. The more you read through the Bible, the more you will know God's ways and His will expressed through people.

Psalm 103: 7 He made known his ways to Moses,
  his deeds to the people of Israel:

If you were not raised in a Christian family, or have not been living for God or have recently experienced desire for more of God, get into a Bible class that teaches God's Word with faith.
If you give yourself wholly, completely to God and ask Him for wisdom and understanding, God will teach you things in the scriptures that you can directly apply to your life and can help others to understand.

Covenant

Rather than try to convince you how good God is, I will examine the blessings God spoke to Moses for Israel. They are for Israel. By faith, in Jesus Christ, we are made one with Abraham and Moses. The covenant promises God made to them are for those who believe in Jesus Christ because Jesus completely fulfilled all the laws because he never sinned. Jesus also inherited all the promises of God and covenants and He gives them to us who believe in Him. It is the righteousness of Jesus Christ that gives us access to God and the benefits of the covenants.

Ephesians 2: 8 For it is by grace you have been saved, through faith—and this is not from yourselves, it is the gift of God— 9 not by works, so that no one can boast.

Romans 3: 22 This righteousness is given through faith in[h] Jesus Christ to all who believe. There is no difference between Jew and Gentile, 23 for all have sinned and fall short of the glory of God, 24 and all are justified freely by his grace through the redemption that came by Christ Jesus

PEACE

The greeting of Shalom in Hebrew means wholeness – with nothing missing and nothing broken. It means completeness. It is a blessing that means God's best for you. God's desire towards Israel is expressed throughout all of the Old Testament but especially in Deuteronomy He speaks blessings that will come upon Israel for obeying God and keeping in covenant with God.

Deuteronomy 28: 2 All these blessings will come on you and accompany you if you obey the Lord your God:

3 You will be blessed in the city and blessed in the country.

4 The fruit of your womb will be blessed, and the crops of your land and the young of your livestock—the calves of your herds and the lambs of your flocks.

5 Your basket and your kneading trough will be blessed.

6 You will be blessed when you come in and blessed when you go out.

7 The Lord will grant that the enemies who rise up against you will be defeated before you. They will come at you from one direction but flee from you in seven.

8 The Lord will send a blessing on your barns and on everything you put your hand to. The Lord your God will bless you in the land he is giving you.

9 The Lord will establish you as his holy people, as he promised you on oath, if you keep the commands of the Lord your God and walk in obedience to him. 10 Then all the peoples on earth will see that you are called by the name of the Lord, and they will fear you. 11 The Lord will grant you abundant prosperity—in the fruit of your womb, the young of

your livestock and the crops of your ground—in the land he swore to your ancestors to give you.

12 The Lord will open the heavens, the storehouse of his bounty, to send rain on your land in season and to bless all the work of your hands. You will lend to many nations but will borrow from none. 13 The Lord will make you the head, not the tail. If you pay attention to the commands of the Lord your God that I give you this day and carefully follow them, you will always be at the top, never at the bottom. 14 Do not turn aside from any of the commands I give you today, to the right or to the left, following other gods and serving them.

I examine the scriptures for to make it clear what God s promising.

1. Blessed in all places you go. That means no matter where you God, God's protection will be around you. Whatever you do will prosper and be fruitful. (verse 3)
2. Fertility up on your marriage and family and animals is promised. (verse 4)
3. Both you short supply and immediate supply will grow and be more than enough. (verse 5)
4. You will have travelling mercies. That means while you are traveling, God will have his angels guarding you for safe passage. (verse 6)
5. Anyone who fight against you, God will scatter. That means God will defend you. (verse 7)
6. God will bless your storage such as barns. (verse 8)
7. Whatever you do will have the blessing of God on it. (verse 11)
8. God will establish you as a Holy covenant person, God will prosper you in all areas of your life. (verse 9)
9. God will give you favour, special grace so that no matter what you do you will prosper. (verse 12)

Blessing

Blessing means more than enough. You will have more than enough so you can give. God will so abundantly prosper you in your life that whatever you do will flourish. It is a total coverage for all of your life that God is describing here. For instance, your business, your family life, your relationships, all within your sphere of authority will see God's abundant blessing. It means you will not lack or be without. You will have an overflow of blessings. The kind of joy that comes when a farmer harvests his crops will come to you. You will know the overflow or the abundance as in a feast of celebration.

Deuteronomy 28: 2 All these blessings will come on you and accompany you if you obey the Lord your God:

Prosperity

Once more God's will is for you to prosper and live healthy as well as strong. God wants the blessing of His covenant to be upon all areas of your life and if you wholly give yourself to God, you will experience the realm of the blessing of God that will give you joy, peace, abundance in all areas of your life. Read for yourself the words – God will make you prosperous.

Deuteronomy 30: 9 Then the Lord your God will make you most prosperous in all the work of your hands and in the fruit of your womb, the young of your livestock and the crops of your land. The Lord will again delight in you and make you prosperous, just as he delighted in your ancestors, 10 if you obey the Lord your God and keep his commands and decrees that are written in this Book of the Law and turn to the Lord your God with all your heart and with all your soul.

Please see the goodness of God for yourself by reading all of the book of Deuteronomy. Those promises that were for Israel are also for you. It is not a cheap formula; it is not a get rich scheme. It always was God's will to prosper Adam and Eve. Sin's consequences meant losing the blessings of God because of a loss of relationship with God. The same will be true for you or I. The source of the blessing Is the LORD Jesus Christ. Your relationship with Him is central to the covenant. If you sin against God, you cut yourself off from God and the blessing.

Your View

Living in covenant blessing you will be with people who have the same faith. You will Go to different places you have never gone. You will do things you have not done. Your whole life will be changed. Your focus will be on God and living to honour Him and to offer yourself to help others. You will see things differently. The difference is that you are seeing all things in light of God's goodness. You will magnify God. You will start to believe that anything you do will prosper. Many people, make the decision to complete college or university once they recommit to God. Their understanding changes so that they realize the best way to get a job you enjoy and that pays well is to get a college diploma or university degree.

You will experience a sense of family in a new way. Even if your family was close and loving, you will begin to regard other Christians as brothers and sisters. If you did not have a good family situation, you will learn how real love manifests for instance with Christians helping you move or paint or do tasks that you need help with. You will be able to communicate with people in a new way because Jesus is first. Should you worship God first with all your being, you are going to start loving people. Someone asked Jesus what the most important commandments were. Jesus answered with the words that follow.

Mark 12: 29 "The most important one," answered Jesus, "is this: 'Hear, O Israel: The Lord our God, the Lord is one.[e] 30 Love the Lord your God with all your heart and with all your soul and with all your mind and with all your strength.'[f] 31 The second is this: 'Love your neighbor as yourself.'[g] There is no commandment greater than these."

Your Character

Loving God with all your being is a commandment. In each prayer, in each meeting magnifying God, in each occasion that you celebrate God, you grown more in love with Him. As you are in God's presence you take on God's character. You become like Him. He reveals Himself to you and as He does, you realize He is only more wonderful than you knew.

2 Corinthians 3: 18 And we all, who with unveiled faces contemplate[a] the Lord's glory, are being transformed into his image with ever-increasing glory, which comes from the Lord, who is the Spirit.

Holy Living

Part of the covenant blessing is your remaining a holy servant of God. You will be known by your covenant with God.

Deuteronomy 28: 9 The Lord will establish you as his holy people, as he promised you on oath, if you keep the commands of the Lord your God and walk in obedience to him.

A tree of righteousness

Part of the blessing is that you will be as a tree of righteousness planted by God himself. You will bear fruit and be productive and give glory to God by your existence.

Isaiah 61:   They will be called oaks of righteousness,
   a planting of the Lord
   for the display of his splendor.

Psalm 1: 3 That person is like a tree planted by streams of water,
   which yields its fruit in season
and whose leaf does not wither—
   whatever they do prospers.

John 15: 7 If you remain in me and my words remain in you, ask whatever you wish, and it will be done for you. 8 This is to my Father's glory, that you bear much fruit, showing yourselves to be my disciples.

God will bless you with all areas of your life.

The transformation of a life of living in the curse of sin and its consequences to following God and living in the blessing of God's doesn't happen all at once but it does occur in spurts. The longer that you stay in God's presence, the stronger your transformation will be. Once you experience the goodness of God for yourself and have seen God bring healing and provision in your life, you are going to want to press in more than ever before. You are also going to want to share it with others. If you knew you had the most important thing in life, you would want those you care about to get it also. So you will desire to share Christ with your family and people you meet that do not yet know Jesus.

1 Corinthians 9: 16 For when I preach the gospel, I cannot boast, since I am compelled to preach. Woe to me if I do not preach the gospel! 17 If I preach voluntarily, I have a reward; if not voluntarily, I am simply discharging the trust committed to me. 18 What then is my reward? Just this: that in preaching the gospel I may offer it free of charge, and so not make full use of my rights as a preacher of the gospel.

Keep yourself strong in the Spirit.

Do it with prayer and Bible study and in worship. Buy yourself CD's to worship and Christian DVDs so you can enjoy them. Keep with people of like precious faith. It should occur normally; you will begin to love the Christians in your classes and in your associations. You will start living in a way of joy, peace, prosperity above what you could have imagined. It's the goodness of God.

Galatians 5: 16 I say then, walk in the Spirit, and you shall not fulfill the lust of the flesh. 17 For the flesh lusts against the Spirit, and the Spirit against the flesh. These are in opposition to one another, so that you may not do the things that you please. 18 But if you are led by the Spirit, you are not under the law.

There will be intervals or spurts of growth. You may feel God drawing you closer. It may be a calling to spend more time with Him in prayer or in praise or in worship. As you feel the drawing, so will you experience the joy and celebration of His presence as you give your life to God. He will teach you things you have never known. He will quicken you to use your gifts and talents and use you to help others.

Once you have experienced the goodness of God for yourself, keep pressing in to God. Never stop. If you sin, repent quickly and get right back in there with God.

Ephesians 4: 10 Finally, my brothers, be strong in the Lord and in the power of His might. 11 Put on the whole armor of God that you may be able to stand against the schemes of the devil. 12 For our fight is not against flesh and blood, but against principalities, against powers, against the rulers of the darkness of this world, and against spiritual forces of evil in the heavenly places.

Build up yourself

Ways to strengthen yourself include praying, reading scripture, talking about the things of God in a Bible study, taking a class about God, watching preaching and teaching.

Jude 1: 20 But you, beloved, build yourselves up in your most holy faith. Pray in the Holy Spirit. 21 Keep yourselves in the love of God while you are waiting for the mercy of our Lord Jesus Christ, which leads to eternal life.

Build up your faith

Ephesians 5: 19 Speak to one another in psalms, hymns, and spiritual songs, singing and making melody in your heart to the Lord. 20 Give thanks always for all things to God the Father in the name of our Lord Jesus Christ, 21 being submissive to one another in the fear of God.

The life God has for you is a life of victory. The life God has for you is abundance. God wants to use you, so you can help others. You will start using your spiritual gifts. You will desire to help others. You will start caring about people. You will start desiring to give. Your life will be focused on how you can give and how you can serve rather than just what you can get.

Genesis 12: 2 "I will make you into a great nation,
    and I will bless you;
I will make your name great,
    and you will be a blessing.[a]

Prayer

There are different ways to teach prayer. There are whole books and volumes of books on prayer. I am explaining the type of praying with understanding that is in my book Kinds of prayer. Search the scriptures. Find strong scriptures about the things you are praying about. It could be health, finances, purchases etc. As you search either a Strong's concordance or an on line search engine for scriptures, either write them or type them.

Use those scriptures to literally pray over yourself. Example.

More than a conqueror

Romans 8: 37 No, in all these things we are more than conquerors through Him who loved us

"Thank you God that I am more than a conqueror through Christ who loved me" You are literally praying God's will for your life. It is a scripture that shows God's desire for you to be not just a conqueror but more than a conqueror. As you pray it, also receive it over your life. As you hear the words, absorb them with your spirit. Praying scriptures and confessing them will help you to live a victorious life. The words of your mouth must come into agreement with what God says about you in His Word.

Words

Literally pray "Holy Spirit set a guard over my mouth. Keep a watch over the door of my lips. |
Psalm 141: 3 Set a guard over my mouth, Lord;
    keep watch over the door of my lips.

Psalm 19: 14 May these words of my mouth and this meditation of my heart be pleasing in your sight, Lord, my Rock and my Redeemer.

If you ask the Holy Spirit to help you with this area of your life, He will. He will correct you if you say negative things about yourself or about others. What we say about ourselves or others help shape our thoughts and our reality. Our words should come into alignment with God's Holy Word and what He says about us.

Example, if you make an error don't say "O, you dummy." Instead, Say "God help me to do it correctly." Turn it into a prayer. Rather than insult yourself or someone, ask the Holy Spirit what things you should say.

Read the Word of God; Pray the word of God. Believe the word of God. Live the Word of God.

It's God's desire to strengthen you so you can live your best life possible. God desires for you to know salvation, healing, deliverance and living and abundant life beyond what you could have known. As you Give yourself to God, remember to thank Him. Give Him all the glory.

He always cause you to triumph

2 Corinthians 2: 14
14 Now thanks be to God who always causes us to triumph in Christ and through us reveals the fragrance of His knowledge in every place.

Overcomer through Jesus Christ

Revelation 21: 7 He who overcomes shall inherit all things, and I will be his God and he shall be My son.[c]

Revelation 3: 21 "To him who overcomes will I grant to sit with Me on My throne, as I also overcame and sat down with My Father on His throne.

6 CONCLUSION

Chapter 6

My main purpose for writing the book is so that people could get a book that had the core truths of scriptural blessing for God's people. It is my hope that you have learned that Jesus is Saviour and Lord. Jesus is healer. Jesus is deliverer. God's desire is to give you life you fully enjoy for all the days of your life. Once you experience the goodness of God for yourself, you are going to want to serve Him with all your being.

It is essential that you get connected to a church that preaches and teaches these truths with faith. If you did not know about Christian television, it could be an excellent resource to you. Christian books and materials and study helps as well as sermons and Bible classes will help you to know God more.

If you are the only Christian in your family, it is important that you know there are millions of believers in North America alone – you can connect to others through Christian media and find a Church that believes in the truths taught in my book. You are not alone. You are a member of the body of Christ. It is important to be a part of a church, so you can make friends and learn about your spiritual gifts and use them. Use Christian media to keep you company. Rather than be with people who do not build you up spiritually, watch Christian preaching. It will comfort you because you will feel a spiritual connection with the people.

It doesn't mean you never see non-Christians, but your closest friends should be those who believe in God the way you do. Pray and God will bring you the right people. Pray and ask God to use you to be a blessing to someone else. God can give you ideas of how to help others. For instance, you could help mow someone's lawn or you could shovel snow. These types of things don't require much on your part, but you will be helping someone. You will have opportunity to do something to give God glory.

Different level of living

You can live in the blessing of God living being a contributing member of society. You can also be living in the high calling – the life of God His blessing upon you. Don't settle for less than God's best for your life. There is only way you can get it; it is by giving yourself wholly to God. Should you give yourself: spirit, soul, body to God – He will show himself to be worthy. As you keep pressing towards Jesus, He is right there with you transforming you from glory to glory by His Holy Spirit.

Phil 3: 14 I press toward the goal to the prize of the high calling of God in Christ Jesus.

7 PRAYERS

PRAYERS

The following prayers are samples of prayers you could pray for important reasons. You could pray the same meaning in your own words. The prayers are meant as examples only.

PRAYER FOR SALVATION

Thank you- Jesus that you died for me on the cross. Thank you that you rose from the dead and ascended into heaven. Thank you that you are coming back again. I thank you Jesus for forgiving my sins. Thank you for your blood that cleanses me from all sin and unrighteousness. Thank you that your blood makes me holy. Thank you for saving me. Fill me with the Holy Spirit to overflowing. I pray for the baptism of the Holy Spirit. Lead me to other people who love you and serve you and that can help me know more about you. Give me the discerning of spirits strong. I thank you and praise you. With my mouth, I confess Jesus Christ is my LORD. Amen.

PRAYER FOR BAPTISM OF THE HOLY SPIRIT

Thank you- Jesus that you promised to send the gift of the Holy Spirit to us. Thank you that this promise is to all believers. I am a believer. I want all of you that you will give me. I want to know you God. Baptize me in the Holy Spirit with the evidence of speaking in other tongues. I believe you want to fill me to overflowing with your Spirit so that I might be an effective witness for Christ on the earth. Thank you for saving me. Thank you for your Holy presence. [begin praising God for what He has done for you – sing worship choruses and praise God in your natural language. Believe that He is present with you – start praising and worshipping Him. As phrases come to you in other tongues, say them – praise God with new tongues.] I praise you. I thank you. I receive the baptism of the Holy Spirit.

PRAYER FOR RELEASING ANGELS

God, I thank you that angels are ministering spirits sent as ministers to us. I pray over my prayer request NAME IT HERE. God I pray release angels to perform it. I thank you for releasing the answer to me. I praise you for it. Amen.

PRAYER FOR RESISTING EVIL

I am the redeemed of the LORD. Jesus Christ has saved me. I am a new creation in Christ Jesus. Jesus blood covers me. I live in the spirit. The Holy Spirit of God fills my spirit. O Holy Spirit quicken me; give me wisdom. Pray [expecting God will give you discerning of spirits so you will have the right words to speak.]

In the name of Jesus Christ, I bind you. I rebuke you evil spirit. In the name of Jesus, I command you to go out. You have no place in my life. I cast you out. You have no place with me. I am covered by the blood of Jesus and His righteousness is my righteousness. Go out evil spirit in the name of Jesus Christ!

Thank you, Holy Spirit for your holy presence. Release angels to drive out the enemy. Thank you. Amen.

PRAYER FOR PROTECTION

Holy Spirit release angels to protect me. I plead the blood of Jesus over me. I pray the protection you promise to your people. Cover me Jesus. Holy Spirit give me wisdom, discernment and understanding. Thank you for angels that guard over me. Thank you for your blood that protects me and a hedge of protection around me. I praise you O God. [praise God with some worship choruses and expect God's holy presence to be manifest in you]. Thank you. O God for protection.

PRAYER FOR HEALING

Lord Jesus, Thank you that you gave your life for me so that I can be saved, healed and delivered. I thank you for the scripture that by your stripes I am healed. I thank you for my healing.

NAME THE DISEASE I bind you in the name of Jesus. I cast you out. I pray over myself that I would be whole spirit, soul and body.

Thank you, God. for your healing manifestation in my life. I give you all the glory. Amen.

PRAYER OF REPENTENCE

Jesus, thank you for your blood shed for me. I repent of the sin of NAME IT. I thank you for liberty from sin. I cut off the root of iniquity in my family. I thank you for your empowering presence to live a Holy life. Holy Spirit lead and guide me in the paths of righteousness. Thank you for giving me godly desires. Let my life align with your word. In Jesus name. Amen.

Prayer of dedication as a giver

God, thank you for prospering me. Let me be a giver you can use to give to others. God let my character be humble and giving so that you place things and wealth in my hands and I will give as you lead me. If you prosper me with more than enough, I will obey your promptings to give to the gospel, to people and for the glory of God. Use me as a giver. I give myself wholly to you. In Jesus name. Amen.

Prayer for deliverance

Jesus, I thank you I can speak with you my Saviour and my LORD. I renounce sin and the addiction of NAME IT. Your word says that who you set free stays free in Jesus. I need you to help me. I plead your blood over me. In the name of Jesus I rebuke you sin of NAME IT. You have no place in me! My body is a temple of the Holy Spirit. Holy Spirit teach me and quicken the scriptures to me so that I may live in the spirit.

Jesus, By faith I ask you to connect me with strong believing Christians who can help me to live a holy life. Thank you. Amen.

OTHER BOOKS BY
CHRIS A. LEGEBOW

Available on Amazon.ca Amazon.com or Kindle
Or the Create Space webstore.

By Living Word Publishers

Angels: Ministering Spirits

An Excellent Spirit: Living Life Wholly Unto God

Covenant With God: God's Relationship With Man

Discovering and Using your Spiritual Gifts

Divine Healing in the Scriptures: God's Mercy Towards Man

Jesus Christ: Saviour, Healer, Deliverer, LORD

Kinds of Giving: From the Holy Scriptures

Signs of Jesus Coming

Spheres of Authority: Know yours

The Commandments

The Doctrine of Christ: Essential Truths of Scripture

Continued…

OTHER BOOKS BY
CHRIS A. LEGEBOW

The Five-Fold Ministry: Gifts to the Church

Kinds of Prayer. Knowing Them and Using Them Effectively

Living Life Fully: Knowing your Purpose

The Anointing: the Glory of God

The High Calling: Life Worth Living

The Sacraments: A Charismatic Guide

ABOUT THE AUTHOR

Chris Legebow is a Christian Professor of English and Communications. She has taught at the elementary, high school and College and University levels. She has ministered in her local churches in intercessory prayer, teaching Sunday school and other Christian Doctrine classes to children and youth. She has preached to congregations and given her testimony. Although she was not raised in a Christian home, she came to know Jesus Christ as her Saviour and LORD while she was studying in University. This radically transformed her life in terms of priorities and commitment.

She has a strong passion for the great commission – that Jesus Christ would be preached throughout all the earth believing that it a major sign of the LORD's return. She has been a part of several different types of full gospel charismatic churches but has also gained much of her insight and enlightenment from Christian Media and broadcasting. She hopes to continue ministering, serving, interceding and giving and teaching until the LORD returns.